Breed Lover's Guide™

GREYHOUND

A Practical Guide for the Greyhound Lover

Cindy Victor

Greyhound

Project Team
Editor: Stephanie Fornino
Indexer: Lucie Haskins
Design: Mary Ann Kahn

T.F.H. Publications, Inc.
One TFH Plaza
Third and Union Avenues
Neptune City, NJ 07753

T.F.H. Publications
President/CEO: Glen S. Axelrod
Executive Vice President: Mark E. Johnson
Publisher: Christopher T. Reggio
Production Manager: Kathy Bontz

Printed and bound in China
10 11 12 13 14 15   1 3 5 7 9 8 6 4 2

Library of Congress Cataloging-in-Publication Data
Victor, Cindy.
  Greyhound / Cindy Victor.
      p. cm.
  Includes index.
  ISBN 978-0-7938-4175-2 (alk. paper)
  1. Greyhound. I. Title.
  SF429.G8V53 2010
  636.753'4--dc22
                                2009042966

This book has been published with the intent to provide accurate and authoritative information in regard to the subject matter within. While every precaution has been taken in preparation of this book, the author and publisher expressly disclaim responsibility for any errors, omissions, or adverse effects arising from the use or application of the information contained herein. The techniques and suggestions are used at the reader's discretion and are not to be considered a substitute for veterinary care. If you suspect a medical problem consult your veterinarian.

Note: In the interest of concise writing, "he" is used when referring to puppies and dogs unless the text is specifically referring to females or males. "She" is used when referring to people. However, the information contained herein is equally applicable to both sexes.

The Leader In Responsible Animal Care For Over 50 Years!™
www.tfh.com

Table of Contents

Chapter 1

History of
the Greyhound

The Greyhound is the fastest dog on earth and a breed for the ages. Since antiquity, Greyhounds have been prized for their grace, speed, and beauty. Immortalized in the art and writings of many cultures, the Greyhound is also the only dog breed mentioned in the Bible (Proverbs 30:29-31, King James Version).

But grace, speed, and beauty don't explain why 20,000 retired racing Greyhounds are adopted into loving homes each year in the United States alone. And we don't love them just because they are quiet dogs who smell clean, shed little, and are easy to groom. No, we love our Greyhounds for their calm and gentle nature, their playfulness, and the fact that every Greyhound we meet could inspire a book. Still, we admit to being mesmerized by their beauty and the array of colors in which they come. From his refined muzzle to the tip of his long, curved tail, the Greyhound exemplifies elegance of form. This is a gorgeous dog, and he gives the impression that he knows it. His look says "I am here to melt your heart. You are here to give me biscuits and take me on car rides. Let's get going!"

The Greyhound's Ancient Origins

What a history Greyhounds have to share! As early as 3000 BCE, Pharaoh Menes I—in addition to unifying Upper and Lower Egypt—was breeding the first pedigrees: Afghan Hounds, Salukis, and Greyhounds. Tomb paintings of Greyhounds date from before 2000 BCE. Yet even before Menes I went to all that effort, a painted terra-cotta bowl ringed with Greyhounds was fashioned by an anonymous ceramicist (Bowl with Dog Pattern, Susa I epoch circa 4000 BCE). The Greyhounds are lying on their bellies, their fannies not touching the ground. Necessitated by their physique, the peculiar posture is an endearing pose that today brings a smile to thousands of Greyhound owners.

Greyhounds are beloved for their gentle nature and playfulness.

WHAT IS A BREED CLUB?

A breed club is an association of fanciers of a specific dog breed. With the purpose of preserving and protecting the breed, the club writes the breed standard, maintains a stud book, provides information to the public about the breed, helps people find a reputable breeder, and sponsors dog shows and other events related to the breed. Clubs may also raise funds for research on breed-specific health issues.

In the 1st century CE, the Roman poet Ovid wrote about Greyhounds in *Metamorphoses*, while across the Mediterranean, in Egypt, Queen Cleopatra enjoyed watching her Greyhounds compete in what we now call open field coursing—a sport in which dogs race in pursuit of live game. Had Cleopatra been born later, I'm sure she would have approved of the Forest Laws that were established in the early 11th century by King Canute to ensure that only noblemen could own and hunt with Greyhounds.

Coming to the New World

Greyhounds came to the New World with Spanish explorers in the 1500s and were in the colonies by the time of America's war for independence in 1776. This was followed by the importation of more Greyhounds to North America from England and Ireland for use in controlling wild game during the development of the American West. While camping in Indian territory, General George Armstrong Custer wrote about his beloved Greyhounds and slept with the one he called Byron. Greyhounds even played a part in the California Gold Rush. They were used as lead dogs for at least one wagon, as reported by *The Wyoming Telescope* in 1859.

The Contemporary Greyhound

Roger Caras, for years the host of the annual Westminster Kennel Club Dog Show and president of the American Society for the Prevention of Cruelty to Animals (ASPCA), owned Greyhounds and wrote with love and respect for the breed. What was most remarkable to Caras is that the breed hasn't changed much since long-ago times. For all of his globetrotting, the Greyhound has remained true to type. Concurring with Caras is Corky Vroom, an American Kennel Club (AKC) all-breed handler, who for decades was recognized by millions of viewers of the Westminster show. Writing for the Greyhound Club

WINNING AT WESTMINSTER

The breed with the most consecutive Hound Group wins in Westminster Kennel Club shows is the Greyhound, with seven wins in the 1930s. In the 1940s, Champion Magic of Mardormere took Best in Group three years in a row. Champion Aroi Talk of the Blues was group winner in 1978 and 1980.

of America (GCA), Vroom noted that "The breed is really a classic one; fads have not affected it that much. People come along and try to change the [Greyhound's] type—it has its vogue, but never really affects the breed."

The Kennel Club (KC), founded in England in 1870, sums up the Greyhound's character as "possessing remarkable stamina and endurance"; its temperament as "intelligent, gentle, affectionate and even-tempered"; and its general appearance as including "a suppleness of limb, which emphasise in a marked degree its distinctive type and quality." Not incidentally, the KC presents the world's largest dog show, Crufts, which had its debut in 1891. But for Greyhound lovers, the most exciting Crufts show was in 1934, when a Greyhound named Southball Moonstone took Best in Show.

Racing Greyhounds

Greyhound racing as a legalized business exists throughout most of the world. Greyhound-Data (www.greyhound-data. com), a database containing Greyhound

pedigrees and race results worldwide, currently lists close to 700 breeding kennels in Ireland, the United Kingdom, Australia, New Zealand, and the United States—with Ireland having the most and the United States having the fewest. Hundreds more exist throughout Europe, South America, Africa, and the Middle East. In countries where betting on Greyhound racing is illegal, racing still exists as a spectator sport.

In the United States there is tremendous dissension on whether Greyhound racing should be allowed to continue or be banned. But whether one is for, against, or neutral, everyone involved in Greyhound adoption shares a love for the breed. And with approximately 300 adoption groups working throughout the country to find homes for these dogs, you will find your wonderful retired racer.

Therapy Work

Many retired racers, in addition to becoming pampered pets, play other roles in society. For one thing, Greyhounds make excellent therapy dogs. (See Chapter 8: Activities With Your

For all of his globetrotting, the Greyhound has remained true to type.

Greyhound.) Following the September 11, 2001, attack on America, Greyhounds were among the therapy dogs who provided comfort to rescue workers and to families awaiting news of loved ones near Ground Zero.

Blood Donation

Retired racers help save the lives of other dogs by being universal blood donors. Dogs have a variety of blood types, which are called dog erythrocyte antigens, or DEA. Dogs who test negative for DEA 1.1, as well as the majority of other blood types, are universal blood donors. Other breeds can meet this criterion, but because veterinary teaching hospitals can arrange for newly retired racers to be housed at the hospital for a period of time and because Greyhounds are easy to work with, they are known for filling this need. Many are adopted while at the hospital and are brought back to make donations; others go on to an adoption group and from there into a loving home.

Prison Foster Programs

Prison foster programs for retired racers have been developed in several states. After retiring and being assessed for compatibility with children, small dogs, and cats, the Greyhounds live in a

LURE COURSING

—Laurel Drew, breeder, trainer, and archivist for the
Greyhound Club of America (GCA)

Lure coursing was invented in the 1970s so that people with sighthounds (hounds who hunt by sight rather than scent) could participate in coursing without killing. Open field coursing always included the possibility of the hounds killing the hare. (Hares are not little cottontails; they are about the size of a Whippet and as fast as a horse.) Lure coursing is done with a lure, usually a white plastic garbage bag tied to a string (shark line) and laid out on a field around a set of pulleys to imitate how a hare might run. A motor drags the lure around the course, and the hounds pursue the lure. Greyhounds are especially adept at this sport, and most of them love it. Before participating, make sure that your dog is in good condition. This is a strenuous sport but one in which you can watch your Greyhound run as he was born to do.

correctional facility with inmates who have been trained as handlers. While in the program, the dogs' time is filled with exercise, basic obedience training, and socialization as they accompany their handlers everywhere they go. Inmates keep a journal of their charge's daily activities, which is given to the new owner upon the dog's adoption. Often, inmates and adopters correspond about the Greyhounds who have enriched their lives. This truly is a situation in which everyone benefits.

Of Kings, Queens, and Presidents

Greyhounds have been a favorite of royalty and dignitaries throughout the ages. King Richard II of England owned Greyhounds, and so did Queen Victoria. Frederick the Great of Prussia was buried beside his 11 female Greyhounds at Sans Souci Palace. Abraham Lincoln had a Greyhound on his family's coat of arms. Rutherford B. Hayes, 19th president of the United States, said on the death of his Greyhound, Grim, "The whole country knew him, and respected him."

Greyhounds in Literature

Works of timeless writers such as Dante, Chaucer, and Shakespeare refer to Greyhounds. In Homer's epic poem *The Odyssey*, the Greyhound Argus—just a puppy when Odysseus began his 20-year odyssey—not only waits to see his master again before dying but is the only being who recognizes Odysseus on his return home.

Less noble but happier were the Greyhounds owned by the English Reverend James Woodforde, who in 1786 recorded in his diary that one of his Greyhounds, Jigg, "go in and ate the whole Charter, with a Cold Tongue." Apparently, the poor reverend didn't learn to train his dogs. In 1794, he recorded that another of his Greyhounds, Fly, "ran away with a Shoulder of Mutton."

Have we as Greyhound owners changed throughout our dogs' history? Certainly we're more protective of our beautiful companions and more knowledgeable about their health needs. And inasmuch as you and I don't have countries to run and territorial wars to fight, we have time to meet our Greyhounds' needs. Still, I like to think that Cleopatra gave tummy rubs.

Greyhounds have been a favorite of royalty and dignitaries throughout the ages.

TIMELINE

- 1014: Britain enacts Forest Laws prohibiting serfs and slaves from owning Greyhounds.
- 1500s: Greyhounds are brought to America by Spanish explorers.
- 1776: The passion of Elizabeth I for coursing results in the first modern coursing club.
- 1907: The Greyhound Club of America (GCA) is formed.
- 1912: Owen Patrick (O.P.) Smith invents the mechanical lure and four years later builds a Greyhound racetrack in Emeryville, California. The rest is history!

Chapter 2

Characteristics of Your Greyhound

These sculptural beings called Greyhounds are long of neck, leg, and muzzle. They are sleek and deep chested, with soft fine coats that anyone who likes dogs can't resist petting. They walk with grace. They sleep a lot (16 or more hours a day), often with eyes partially open as if in a trance. When awake, with their doe-like eyes fastened on yours, they ask in their silent Greyhound language: *Isn't it time for a walk? No? Then could we cuddle?*

Living with a Greyhound is in a sense like living with a young child. Both are inquisitive, entertaining, and dependent on Mom or Dad for guidance and care. And protection. Greyhounds literally have thin skin that tears easily. The combination of their single coat of short hair and lack of body fat makes them vulnerable to heatstroke. You—your Greyhound's protector—must make certain that his environment is safe. There can be no exposed nails jutting from the fence in your yard, no leaving him outside in the hot sun. In all weather, he sleeps indoors with you. Your Greyhound will bring you happiness in many ways—and one will be knowing that you are doing your best for him.

The Greyhound's Physical Characteristics

The Greyhound is the archetypical sighthound, and his "type" is recognized throughout the world. Sighthounds, also called "gazehounds," include all hound breeds (including the Afghan Hound, Borzoi, Saluki, and Whippet) that were bred to hunt by sight rather than by scent. National kennel clubs establish "breed standards" to define the ideal dog and help improve the breed with each generation. Greyhounds bred for racing will never be show dogs and are not bred for a specific "look." They differ slightly from show Greyhounds in appearance, but a Greyhound is a Greyhound and

Check It Out

GREYHOUND FAST FACTS

- ✓ **Height:** 23 to 30 (or more) inches (58.5 to 76 cm), depending on sex
- ✓ **Weight:** 50 to 85 pounds (22.5 to 38.5 kg), on average, depending on sex
- ✓ **Coat Type:** Single, short, and smooth
- ✓ **Coat Colors:** So many that anything goes—and they're all gorgeous!
- ✓ **Life Expectancy:** 12 to 14 years

Racing Greyhounds are registered with the National Greyhound Association (NGA).

cannot be anything but beautiful—even if he has a few dings on him from his racing career. Think of them as badges of courage.

Greyhounds registered with the American Kennel Club (AKC) tend to be taller and narrower than their racing counterparts, who are registered with the National Greyhound Association (NGA). AKC dogs also have deeper chests than most racers. Their legs and neck are longer, their backs more arched, and their rear legs more angled. They hold their tails lower as well. NGA Greyhounds have a lot more muscle, especially in the hindquarters, and at racing weight their ribs are visible.

Let's look at some characteristics found in all Greyhounds.

Height and Weight

Males average 26 to 30 inches (66 to 76 cm) at the shoulder and weigh between 65 and 85 pounds (29.5 and 38.5 kg).

OBTAINING A PUPPY OR RETIRED RACER

The overwhelming majority of Greyhounds worldwide are bred for racing. In general, they become available for adoption between two and five years of age. Adoption and rescue groups are found throughout the United States, Canada, Europe, and Australia. There's never a shortage of retired racers to adopt. Not many Greyhounds, though, are bred for show, and this is partly because they are difficult to breed. Females may not come into season until they are two or three, and breeders don't have many males from whom to choose. Mostly, though, it's because Greyhound puppies are a lot to handle. Greyhound litters can be large, with up to a dozen or more pups, all of which are adorable little perpetual motion machines. Still, some brave and energetic souls breed future show Greyhounds. If you're willing to wait for this miracle, as well as travel to get your dog, you will be the happy—if tired—owner of a Greyhound puppy. If, however, you choose to adopt a retired racer, you will have your dog in short time, and he will come to love you as much as would a Greyhound you'd raised from a puppy—probably in a day or two. With many adopted Greyhounds and their owners, love is instantaneous. Dog and adopter look into each other's eyes, and they know.

Females stand 23 to 26 inches (58.5 to 66 cm) tall at the shoulder and weigh 50 to 65 pounds (22.5 to 29.5 kg). Males who weigh in at 90 pounds (41 kg) or more aren't necessarily overweight. We call them "gentle giants."

A Coat of Many Colors

Greyhounds boast a single coat that is short, smooth, and comes in so many colors and color combinations that the AKC standard deems color "immaterial." The American Greyhound Track Operators (AGTO) recognizes 18 colors for NGA dogs. In no particular order, they are: blue, blue brindle, black, black brindle, black and white, fawn, fawn brindle, light red fawn, red fawn, dark red, red brindle, white and black, white and brindle, white and brindle tick, dark brindle, light brindle, brindle, red and white. Every one of them is beautiful to behold, and many more color combinations have been recognized by Greyhound lovers.

The "grey" in "Greyhound" has nothing

A distinguishing feature of the Greyhound is the long, muscular neck.

to do with color, and in Greyhounds, the color gray is called "blue." Blue Greyhounds aren't common in the United States, which makes them highly desirable. You'd have better luck finding a blue Greyhound in Ireland or Australia. Interestingly, peasants in England who were forbidden to hunt in the king's forests tended to prefer brindle and dark colors. Nobles, however, preferred white and lighter colors, which in the forests were easier to see.

Greyhounds tend to go white in the face early on. The red-with-white female whose muzzle is covered with black ticking at age four may have no ticking at all by age seven. The same goes for the brindle male whose face in youth boasted a symmetrical pattern of dark, curving lines. I believe that this early fading of color is a reminder that every day we are graced by a Greyhound's presence is precious. Don't waste a single one!

CHILDREN AND GREYHOUNDS

Greyhounds love people and by nature are gentle, so they're good with children as long as the child is taught how to behave with the dog and to respect his feelings. Any dog will react when handled roughly or teased by children. The reaction can take many forms: a warning growl, a bite, or the dog's becoming fearful of all children. It's not enough that your child knows not to poke, push, or pull on the dog or to let him get loose; children who visit your home must know too. Children must learn not to disturb a Greyhound when he's sleeping or eating and not to feed him anything without your permission. Also explain that holding tight to any part of his body may scare him and that they must not touch him around his eyes, pull his ears, or play with his tail. Reinforce the rules of safety often, and always be aware of what's going on. Never leave babies or young children alone with any dog or give a child sole responsibility for a dog's care—not even for a short while. But do encourage your child to help with the Greyhound's care under your supervision. Greyhounds and children are a wonderful match when the parents are committed to making it so.

Before getting your Greyhound, see whether there are Greyhound "meet and greets" in your vicinity. At these events, which serve to promote Greyhound adoption, you and your child can visit with Greys and their owners. Ask questions. Don't be shy—we love talking about our dogs. And when it's time for you to meet Greyhounds who the adoption group feels would be right for your home, take your child with you to help choose the new family member.

Head

The Greyhound's head is long, narrow, and fairly wide between the ears. The stop (point where a dog's muzzle meets his forehead) is scarcely perceptible. Two distinguishing features are a long muzzle and small, rose-shaped ears that are exquisitely soft to the touch. The ears are thrown back and folded except when the dog is excited; then they open to the sides or reach for the sky.

Eyes can be light or dark, but in most show dogs they're dark. This dates to when Greyhounds of old in England hunted for their owners' food. Dark eyes didn't reflect sunlight and tip prey off that they were being chased. All Greyhounds' eyes are bright and intelligent, showing their great spirit.

Neck and Body

Another distinguishing feature is the long, muscular neck, arching slightly and gradually widening into the shoulders. The chest is deep and the loins well arched. The Grey's "tuck up" gives him the narrow waist that artists love to accentuate. His back—muscular, broad, and long—is what enables him to run so fast. The secret is in the spinal structure, which is much more supple than that of most other breeds. Greyhounds run in a style known as the "double-suspension gallop," or "gait." This is very demanding and can't be maintained for long. That's why Greyhounds are sprinters, not distance runners.

Legs and Feet

The Greyhound's forelegs are straight, set well into the shoulders and turned neither in nor out. Hindquarters are long, muscular, and powerful. Feet are arched and thickly padded, with the two middle toes longer than the two on the outside. This configuration helps the dog grab the ground when running. An interesting bit of anatomy trivia is that on a clear day you

10 REASONS TO ADOPT A GREYHOUND

—Lee Livingood, Certified Dog Behavior Consultant, International Association of Animal Behavior Consultants (IAABC)

1. When you adopt an adult dog, you get to see the adult personality and temperament, which often is different than what you would have seen in the same dog as a puppy. You also get to see the physical characteristics of a full-grown dog.

2. Adult dogs require less work than puppies. Aside from having to be housetrained, puppies teethe, chew, and need much more exercise and attention than adult dogs. Many dogs have the characteristics of puppies until they are well over two years old.

3. Retired racers are low maintenance. They require minimal grooming, and their exercise needs are low to moderate for a dog of their size. Most Greyhounds are naturally laid-back, well mannered, and sensitive. Plus, they're intelligent and respond well to the right training methods.

4. Retired racers adapt to a variety of lifestyles. A retired racer isn't perfect for every family, but he can fit perfectly into almost any lifestyle, as long as you take the time to pick the right retired racer and teach him what he needs to know to be a valued family member.

5. Greyhounds are usually quiet, gentle, and compliant. They blend well into families with well-mannered children. Most Greyhounds love the company of other dogs, and many live happily with cats as well. Some Greyhounds adapt well to homes with very small animals.

6. Greyhounds don't need much exercise. A myth about Greyhounds is that because they're bred to race, they need lots of room to run and constant exercise. But Greyhounds aren't marathon runners; they're sprinters. At the track, they only race every few days. In retirement, a daily walk or two and romping in a fenced yard from time to time are sufficient.

7. Greyhounds are very clean. Their coats are so light and short that grooming is a breeze. Many Greyhounds clean themselves much like cats do. Their coats aren't oily, so they aren't as prone to doggy odor as some breeds are.

8. The average life expectancy of Greyhounds is longer than that of most large breeds: 12 years or more.

9. With nearly 25,000 retired racing Greyhounds available each year, you can "design" your perfect dog. Know what color you want? You can find a Greyhound to match. Know what size you want, from 50 to 100 pounds (22.5 to 45.5 kg)? You can find a racer to fit your needs. Want a couch potato or a fishing buddy? No problem. Need a dog who can live happily in the city? You'll find him. Want a companion for your aging mother? There's one who will fill the bill. Whatever you're looking for, somewhere there is a retired racer waiting to race into your life and heart.

10. Greyhounds are fun. Many adoption groups have an annual reunion picnic and sell the obligatory event T-shirt. One group's T-shirt said it all: "Life with a Greyhound is one big picnic." And that's why most of us have more than one.

might see sunlight through the skin above a Greyhound's calcaneus, or heel bone.

Living With a Greyhound

Before making the great leap into Greyhound ownership, be sure that this is the right breed for you.

Companionability

Greyhounds are good family dogs as long as the children are well behaved. Most Greyhounds get along well with other dogs. (See sidebar "10 Reasons to Adopt a Greyhound" for more information.)

Environment

Greyhounds are sensitive dogs who do best in a calm environment. They're routine oriented and won't thrive without a schedule for the main activities of life: eating, eliminating, exercising, sleeping, and cuddling.

They can adapt to apartments or mansions, but they must live indoors with their family. They're also very sensitive to excessive cold and heat, so if you want a dog who can run free while you're walking in the woods, jump into a lake and swim out to fetch the stick you threw, or trot beside you while you ride your bike, a Greyhound is not for you.

Greyhounds may never be off lead except in a completely enclosed area. There are no exceptions to this rule, as they were bred to hunt by sight and can see 1/2 mile (1 km) into the distance. As much as your dog loves you, when something motivates him to run—the sight of prey or fear of an unfamiliar noise—thousands of years of breeding will kick in, and he'll take off. Calling his name won't stop him; he's going too fast—up to 45 miles (72.5 km) per hour— to even hear you. There is in the Louvre Museum in Paris, France, a marble statue, circa 360 to 350 BCE, of a man and his servant with two Greyhounds. The servant

Playing with your Greyhound is a great way to give him the exercise he needs.

holds the Greyhounds on a leash. Even in ancient times, Greyhound owners knew better than to let their dogs loose.

Exercise Requirements

Although Greyhounds are built to run at high speeds, your new family member doesn't need to run at all. Your car can go 100 miles per hour (161 kph), but for safety's sake you don't drive that fast. Greyhounds need exercise, but a 20-minute walk at least once a day will suffice. If you do let your dog run inside a securely fenced yard, remember three things. He's a retired athlete—not in the shape he was in at the track. He's a sprinter, not a long-distance runner, so a couple of laps around the yard are enough. At the track he ran on a combed, flat surface of sand and clay

Greyhounds are sensitive dogs who do best in a calm environment.

that was monitored for moisture content by full-time employees and kept free of the smallest pebble or twig. Greyhounds love to run, but it's not essential to their well-being, and walking is safer. Besides, what's good for the Greyhound is good for his owner. Not only will a daily walk—or two or three—help you stay fit and trim, but there's another reward to be reaped from walking your Greyhound: A tired dog is a good dog.

Playing indoors is exercise too. After your fast friend has settled in and discovered the joy of stuffed toys, he may make a game of flipping a toy in the air, catching it, and whirling before flipping it again. What fun! Just make sure that he doesn't do this where he can injure himself. Another form of exercise for after he's settled in and bonded with you is tug-of-war, which exercises all of the major muscles in a dog's body. Let him win. He won't feel dominant over you. (However, young children should not play tug-of-war with any dog.)

Health

Greyhounds are healthy dogs but have special health requirements, which we will talk about in Chapter 9. Many people with dog allergies can live comfortably with a Greyhound because of his sleek coat and skin type.

Life Expectancy

The Greyhound's life expectancy is between 12 and 14 years, with some living longer. Consider your Grey a senior at age seven, even though he looks and acts like a young dog. Exercise him, but avoid letting him break into a full-out run. If necessary, shorten his walks as he ages. Senior Greyhounds need to keep their weight up, so don't opt for a low-protein senior diet. Routine checkups, good nutrition, and dental hygiene will help keep your Greyhound in good health and feeling well into old age.

Trainability

Greyhounds are smart dogs who are quite trainable as long as their trainer uses positive methods. (See Chapter 6: Training Your Greyhound.)

Watchdog Ability

Because of the Greyhound's sweet and trusting nature, he's not likely to be a guard dog. Some bark in happy excitement when the doorbell rings, but most just wag their tails while hoping that the visitor has brought treats.

To ensure that a Greyhound is right for you, measure the breed's characteristics against those of your family. Greyhounds are gentle, quiet, intelligent, and sensitive. Allowing them to run loose or run long distances imperils their life. Although easy to train, they do need training. Lee Livingood, recognized by Greyhound lovers as a Greyhound trainer exemplar, said it best: "Training isn't about obedience as much as it's about forming a trusting relationship and establishing a way to communicate."

Chapter
3

Supplies for
Your Greyhound

Whether you adopt a very young Greyhound, an adult dog fresh off the track, or one who's been fostered by an adoption volunteer, bringing baby home is the start of a joyful journey for you and your dog. To ensure a smooth transition for your Greyhound, have ready in advance all of the supplies required for his comfort, health, and safety. This will help him adjust quickly to his new surroundings and lifestyle, and you won't have to dash out on shopping errands. That means less stress for you both and more time for getting to know each other.

Attire and Accessories

I haven't yet met a Greyhound who doesn't love to romp in fresh snow. If my dogs are only going to be outside for a few minutes and there's snow on the ground but the air temperature isn't bitter cold, I don't make them wear coats. But with thin hair and very little body fat, Greyhounds chill easily, so a winter or wet climate calls for appropriate clothing that's designed for Greyhounds, as any other won't be a good fit. If all you need is a light jacket, your dog will be comfortable wearing a sweater or "tummy warmer." This slips over his head and covers his midsection but not his neck. Very cold weather calls for a coat, which may have a snood, a covering for the neck and ears. Most likely he'll shake his ears free of the snood, and you'll return from your walk with a warm dog sporting icicle ears. This is okay if the weather isn't bitter cold and the walk is short. For frigid weather you can get a separate snood that goes higher over the head and tucks under the snood attached to the coat. My dogs can't shake free of this arrangement, so they sigh and forgive me.

You may also want to purchase "pajamas" for your Greyhound if you

Check It Out

SUPPLIES CHECKLIST

- ✓ dog brush or hound mitt
- ✓ dog crate or baby gate
- ✓ doggy nail clippers
- ✓ doggy toothbrush and toothpaste
- ✓ food and water bowls
- ✓ identification (ID tag)
- ✓ martingale collar and 6-foot (1-m) leash
- ✓ outdoor wear as needed
- ✓ squawker to recall loose dog
- ✓ toys and chewies
- ✓ washable dog bed

turn the thermostat way down at night to save on heating costs. Conversely, if you don't give a liver biscuit about the high cost of energy and crank the air conditioner up on summer nights, your Grey's jammies (usually prewashed flannel or cotton–poly-blend fabric) will keep the chill off him. Whether dressing your dog for a walk in the snow or for a costume party, be sure that the attire fits comfortably and isn't too snug for your barrel-chested fashion plate.

Numbing cold may also call for booties or moccasins that are made for Greyhounds and extend higher up the leg than do regular dog boots. Boots shouldn't be worn in soft snow, though, because snow that gets inside a boot can turn to ice between the toes. Ouch!

Baby Gate

A baby gate will confine your Greyhound to a specific room of the house, keep him from going into a room you don't want him in, and restrain him from going up or down stairs. A gate is an extremely useful tool for your dog's safety and your sanity, and it's essential if you don't want to crate your dog.

Your Greyhound's bed should be well cushioned and comfortable.

Bed

Your dog's bed should be well cushioned, have a washable cover, and be big enough to allow him to stretch out. Dogs like to dig in a bed before lying down, so get one that can withstand this treatment. Well-made beds can be found in pet supply and discount stores, pet supply catalogs, and online. You'll probably want two beds, one for your bedroom and one for the family area. And I'd wager a box of dog biscuits that in time you'll want more.

Collar

Only the martingale collar—also known as a Greyhound collar—is safe for walking your Greyhound. It's designed to keep him from backing out of the collar and getting loose, which happens when a dog's neck is as large or larger than his head. A martingale collar gently tightens up so that it won't slip over the dog's ears. It also won't damage fur or hurt his trachea. Most adoption groups send dogs home with a martingale collar and matching leash, also called a lead, and most Greyhound owners find themselves buying at least one fancy martingale for dress-up. Your Greyhound doesn't need a collection of chic collars, but through the ages it's been hard for Greyhound owners to resist putting a stylish collar on that graceful neck. *The Hunt of Maximilian*, a tapestry made in the early 1530s of wool, silk, gold, and silver, shows a black-and-white Greyhound proudly setting off for the imperial hunt wearing an exquisitely embroidered collar. I've seen collars like it at Greyhound picnics.

Indoors, you may choose to have your Grey wear a flat-buckle collar or a quick-release collar. The latter, also called a breakaway collar, is designed to prevent

Only the martingale collar is safe for walking your Greyhound.

SETTING UP A DAILY SCHEDULE

No dog is more used to a regimented life than the racing Greyhound. A daily schedule will comfort your dog as he adjusts to his new environment, give him confidence that he's doing his job, and increase his trust in you. What makes his regimen all the more wonderful is being praised for doing everything on the schedule. When he goes to the bathroom, he's a good boy. When he licks his bowl clean or has his teeth brushed, he's a good boy. How could he not have confidence in himself when he knows what is expected of him and knows that he's up to the task?

strangulation if the collar catches on something. Do not take a Greyhound outside to the fenced yard—even for a quick potty—without his collar and ID tags. Logic may tell you that your dog can't possibly get loose from a fenced yard with a locked gate. But sometimes logic steps aside while the impossible happens, and we learn a sad lesson.

For a proper fit, you should be able to insert at least two fingers between your dog's collar and his neck, whether the collar is martingale, quick release, or flat buckle. Test the martingale indoors to make sure that it is properly fitted before going out. When you walk in front of your dog, pulling gently on the leash, the collar should not begin to slide over his ears.

Crate

Racing Greyhounds live in crates, and while having a dog crate in the home is optional, I wouldn't be without one for each of my dogs. A crate is useful when introducing a dog to his new surroundings. After that it's a cozy home within a home where your dog is safe and secure when he has to be confined. Greyhounds sleep a lot, so leaving your dog crated for a few hours—but not all day—isn't a problem. The crate must be large enough for him to stand up and turn around with ease. Wire crates give the dog a good view of his surroundings, but plastic crates with cutouts for air circulation and a wire door are easier to clean and more den-like. There also are soft-sided crates on the market. They look nice with their zippered mesh doors and large storage pockets, and they're easy to set up and carry for dog shows. However, a Greyhound can chew right through the mesh, so for safety's sake choose between the wire and plastic crates.

My dogs love their plastic crates (which surprises a few friends who prefer wire

A flat buckle collar may be used when your Greyhound is indoors.

snuggly quilt can be added. Anything you put into the crate for your dog to lie on should be washable. Don't put carpet made from long strings in a crate because a bored or anxious dog may chew on his bedding and swallow strings, which can wrap through his intestines. Anything a dog ingests that can't be passed must be surgically removed.

crates or don't crate at all). Our crates are in the family room, which opens to the kitchen. The dogs are crated when left home alone—which never exceeds four hours. Minnie's crate is also her feeding station, to keep her from gobbling down her meal and then eating some of Bruce's, which my sweet boy would let her do. Treats are also given in the crates a number of times a day, so when I say "Kennel up!" the dogs rush to the crates in happy anticipation. They also play musical crates, and the most fun is when I tell them to kennel and both dogs run into the same crate. What I especially like about plastic crates, besides their being cozy and den-like, is that they offer less chance of a collar or tag getting caught on anything. However, wire crates do provide better air circulation, so if you don't have a means of keeping your home cooled in the hot summer months, a wire crate may be the better choice for your dog.

Buy a dog bed that fits the crate, or purchase a pad made for dog crates. A

Exercise Pen

An exercise pen, also called an ex-pen, can be useful but isn't essential. It will confine your dog to where you want him, but if it isn't anchored, he might move it, lift it and crawl out from under it, or attempt to jump over it. Don't confine a dog recovering from neutering to an ex-pen or leave a dog in an ex-pen outdoors unless you are there to supervise. And never confine a Greyhound anywhere by tethering or chaining him. Should he jump in alarm or try to run, disaster could ensue.

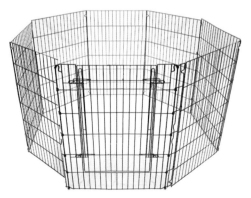

FIRST-AID KIT FOR HIKING AND CAMPING

—Rodger Barr, DVM

No hiking or camping trip with your Greyhound should be without a complete first-aid kit. Before you go, be sure that your dog's flea and tick preventive is up to date. Keeping your dog on leash will prevent the worst imaginable consequences should he run off. It will also keep you from needing to use many of the items listed below.

- antibiotics for infections
- antihistamines such as Benadryl and/or Prednisone for allergic reactions to insect bites, which may cause rapidly developing respiratory distress and death
- bell, to be placed around your dog's collar, to warn and frighten unsuspecting wild animals
- have good access to water, or bring along gallon (4-l) jugs of water—in the event of overheating, you can cool your pet down before his body temperature causes irreparable damage
- metronidazole for nonspecific diarrheas
- nail trimmer and styptic powder (or silver nitrate sticks) for cracked or broken nails
- Pepto-Bismol for vomiting
- pliers to pull out porcupine quills—bring tweezers, too
- roll of cotton or cast padding and Vetwrap, along with the knowledge of how to use them in making a bandage or a splint
- staple gun for lacerations and the basic knowledge of how to use one
- tomato juice or Skunk-Off in case of a skunk encounter

Food and Water Bowls

You'll need two large bowls, one for food and one for water. Stainless steel is preferred, as plastic bowls can cause an allergic reaction in dogs, especially if the plastic has been scratched. And ceramic bowls may crack. Both plastic and ceramic bowls, when even slightly cracked, may harbor dangerous bacteria. Be sure to wash the food bowl after each use and the water bowl at least once a day.

Grooming Supplies

You'll need a soft bristle brush or hound mitt to give your Greyhound's coat a daily brushing. You'll also need a doggy toothbrush and chicken- or beef-flavored doggy toothpaste, which your dog will love, so that you can brush his teeth every day, which is critically important. Your Greyhound will seldom need bathing—probably once or twice a year—and you'll want a tearless dog shampoo for this. His nails must be trimmed every week or two. Doggy nail clippers come in two styles: guillotine or scissors. In spite of their scary name, guillotine clippers are easier on both dog and human. Easier still, if your dog will tolerate it, is a "Dremel-type" grinder. (See Chapter 5 for more on keeping your dog's teeth healthy, his coat clean, and his nails trimmed.) Lastly, you'll need a pooper scooper for your yard and a continuous supply of plastic bags for outside your yard. But you knew this. If you weren't a good citizen, you wouldn't adopt a Greyhound!

Identification

Anytime your Greyhound is outside his home he should have attached to his collar an ID tag with your name, address, and phone number; and his rabies and license tags. But collars can be lost or

Stainless steel is a good choice for food and water bowls because it is durable and won't harbor bacteria.

SIGNS YOUR DOG HAS TO POTTY

All puppies need to eliminate often, and retired racers are used to four turnouts a day. But the excitement of a new life and a change in diet may necessitate more outings at first. Whether a puppy or retired racer, your Greyhound may signal his need to go by whining, pacing in circles, vigorously biting on a toy, or going to the door that leads to his grassy bathroom. Barking when he needs to potty is to my mind very thoughtful, as there's no missing that cue.

removed, rendering ID tags useless. Racing Greyhounds are tattooed in each ear to ensure that the correct dog enters each race. But most people don't know how to trace a lost Greyhound by his ear tattoos, and the tattoos can be hard to read. Microchips, however, are permanent and so commonly used now that most shelters and veterinarian clinics are able to scan a lost dog to find where he belongs. The microchip is a tiny transmitter that's inserted by syringe under the skin over the dog's shoulders. It's not painful and won't cause an allergic reaction. You'll be given a chip number that you can register into a lost-pet Internet database. This enables the finder of a lost pet to locate his owner.

Leash

You'll want a 6-foot (2-m) nylon, hemp, or leather leash. Don't let anyone talk you into getting an adjustable-length, retractable leash. (They retract with the push of a button.) Your Grey could pull it out of your hand, and the noise of it hitting the ground would spook him into running. Unable to shake free of the thing, he would not stop. Be wary, too, of other dogs on retractable leashes. If a dog on a retractable leash should try to interact with your Greyhound, the leash can make your dog very nervous. If it wraps around your dog's leg, he can be severely injured.

Muzzle

Your adoption group may provide you with a plastic muzzle. Your dog wore a muzzle when he raced and during turnouts (potty breaks) with other dogs. This is a safety device and good to use when introducing your Greyhound to small children or other dogs or pets for the first time. A muzzle is also useful if your dog has a boo-boo that needs to be tended to at home. As much as your Greyhound loves you, he may snap if you are changing his dressing and it hurts a little. When I was in this situation with my Minnie, I brought out the muzzle I'd been given by our adoption group when we adopted her several years earlier. She hadn't worn a muzzle in all the time she'd been with us. Yet when I came toward her holding it, she thrust her head into it with apparent excitement. "Where's the race?" she seemed to be asking with assurance that she would win. So keep a muzzle handy in case it's needed. But don't ever leave your dog alone wearing a muzzle. He can't get it off by himself, and if it were to catch on something, he could be injured in his struggle to get free.

Squawker

A squawker is a predator call that makes the sound of a hare or other animal in distress. Racing kennel operators and trainers use squawkers to recall dogs after a race. They are available at sporting goods stores and from such online sources as the National Greyhound Association (NGA). Every Greyhound owner should have a squawker in case her

Your adoption group may provide you with a muzzle, which is a safety device; ex-racing Greyhounds are accustomed to them.

Greyhounds become chilled easily, so in cooler or wet weather, they may need to wear clothing to keep warm.

Grey gets loose. Although there are other ways to lure him back if he is still within range of seeing and hearing you, when he is beyond that range the squawker will be one of the best purchases you ever made. I learned this from experience after ten years of owning Greyhounds and now keep squawkers by the doors to my fenced yard and garage and another in my car.

Some squawkers are operated by a shake of the hand; these are very sensitive to touch and great to have near the door

or in the car. Others that you blow like a whistle are smaller and more convenient to have on your person when out with your dog. Whichever squawker you choose, test it on your dog to make sure that he reacts—there are some who won't. After testing it, don't use it again unless it's necessary. You don't want to make a toy of the squawker, which would greatly reduce its effect on your dog. Do buy at least one squawker. My loose Greyhound was chasing a neighbor dog, and they both quickly disappeared, running toward

Racing kennel operators and trainers use squawkers to recall dogs after a race.

a nature preserve. I shook the squawker once and Bruce came running home. One caveat, though: Don't use a squawker if your dog must run through traffic to get to you.

Toys and Chewies

For Greyhounds the stuff of everyday life definitely includes "stuffies"–stuffed toys that ideally squeak, squawk, scream, or moo when bitten. Some Greyhounds treat their stuffies with the tenderness of a child holding or sleeping with a favorite doll. My Bruce is one, rarely going from here to there without a stuffie in his mouth and never sleeping without one. But many Greyhounds vigorously shake

their stuffies, toss them in the air with great joy, and even rip them open. A stuffie injured in play should be removed to your "home hospital" until you have time to restuff and sew it up. (Dental floss holds up better than thread.) And don't give a stuffie to a puppy, who will surely tear it apart and perhaps swallow a piece of stuffing.

Durable rubber toys are safe for your Greyhound, but the product must state that the rubber is durable. Soft rubber is dangerous, as your dog is a strong chewer. Small pieces that he bites off of a nondurable toy can lodge in his throat or intestine. Also beware of toys with plastic parts or dangling strings that can be torn off and swallowed.

Any toy or chew you give your dog should be too large for him to swallow. Nylabone chews of the right size for your pup are virtually indestructible and are often recommended for Greyhounds. My Minnie and I have great fun playing with Nylabone's rubber tug toy. It isn't durable rubber, but Minnie isn't chewing it, and I don't leave her alone with it. (I do let her win every time, but she doesn't know this.) A tug-of-war rope toy may be acceptable under supervision, but don't leave your dog alone with it for even

a minute. Pantyhose, socks, and that dreadful fringed scarf you bought on sale are definitely not dog toys!

Some retired racers who are adopted fresh from the track, without being fostered first, may not have had experience with toys. If your new pup is one, he may not understand why you are giving him a stuffie or chewy. Give him time. He'll catch on.

If you judge every purchase you make for your new Greyhound by its safety, quality, and ability to add to his well-being—or by the comfort and pleasure it will give him—you won't go wrong.

Chapter
4

Feeding
Your Greyhound

Put a dozen dedicated Greyhound owners in a room to talk about Greyhound nutrition and you'll get a half-dozen opinions on what constitutes the optimal diet for a Greyhound. And all may be right. We have choices in what to feed our dogs but only one goal: good health and long life for our Greys!

Food Basics

Basic to a dog's diet are carbohydrates, fats, proteins, vitamins, minerals, and water. Too little or too much of any of these or getting them from the wrong sources can harm his health. Fortunately, we—not the food manufacturers and not our dogs—are in charge of what goes into the bowl.

Carbohydrates

"Carbs" come from grains, sugars, fruits, and vegetables. They supply energy and assist with body functions such as temperature regulation and digestion. Because they are a less expensive source of energy than proteins or fats, many dog foods contain more carbs than our dogs need. A balanced dog food will have about 50 percent carbohydrates. Most foods have corn, soy, rice, potato, or wheat as their primary carbohydrates. A top-quality brand may not include corn or soy, and any diet fit for your Greyhound will not include cheap feed, known as "filler." Filler contributes little or no nutritional value to the food.

Fats

Fats are a concentrated source of energy and also contribute to a dog's coat, skin, connective tissue, and kidney health. They make food taste better too. But go easy, as too much fat can cause pancreatitis. This is a severe inflammation of the pancreas, an organ that aids in

The right amount of fats in the diet contributes to a healthy, shiny coat.

Puppy Love

THE RETIRED RACER'S EARLY DIET

Because most Greyhounds begin life on a Greyhound farm and then are moved to a racing kennel, let's look at what they eat at their first "homes." At about four weeks, puppies are being weaned and are fed three meals a day. The meals may consist of baby food, such as rice cereal, and powdered goat milk. Soon a high-quality, high-protein puppy chow is added, and at eight weeks the pups are getting ground beef and rice, the puppy chow, and vitamins. From about three to six months, they're fed twice daily and get as much high-protein puppy chow and raw beef as they will eat, plus supplements, including calcium, cod liver oil, iron, and vitamin B-12. From six months to a year, they're fed 2 to 3 pounds (1 to 1.5 kg) of food—about half meat and half meal—a day. During a dog's racing career, the ratio is about 70 percent beef and 30 percent meal.

But the retired racer you adopt should not have a high-protein diet, which makers of commercial dog food often label "active adult." Too much protein isn't good for your Greyhound, because as a new member of the Active Couch Potato Club, he can't use it.

digestion of food. Fat trimmings from any kind of meat or poultry should be thrown out, not fed to your Greyhound.

Proteins
Good sources of protein without too much fat are required for a dog's growth and maintenance, but too much protein can harm a Greyhound's kidneys. The adult Greyhound who doesn't participate in high-energy sports such as lure coursing should have a diet with 22 to 27 percent protein. Greys do well on protein from animal sources, so the first ingredient in any dog food you purchase should be a good-quality animal protein.

Vitamins and Minerals
Vitamins and minerals play many roles in a dog's health and are needed to maintain the body's functionality. High-quality dog foods contain sufficient vitamins and minerals for most dogs, but some may benefit from a supplement prescribed by a veterinarian. To feed your Greyhound a home-cooked diet, you must learn how much of each vitamin and mineral is required to meet his needs. This is one reason why it's convenient to feed a top-quality commercial food.

Water
Clean, fresh water should always be available for your Greyhound. Dogs

Racing Greyhounds receive a lot of protein in their diets, but once they retire, they no longer need as much.

dehydrate easily, and dehydration harms kidneys and other organs. Warm weather and exercise increase the need for water, so check often to make sure that the water bowl isn't empty. And never restrict water except on the advice of your veterinarian.

Types of Foods

Keep your Greyhound healthy by feeding him a balanced diet appropriate to his age, activity level, and unique needs. You can do this by feeding him a high-quality commercial or noncommercial diet. You may also use some of one diet and some of another to good effect. This is helpful if your dog is a picky eater and it's hard for you to keep his weight up. In fact, some animal nutritionists believe that pets, like people, should eat a wide variety of foods. They would have you choose two or three dog food products and switch among them periodically. What isn't acceptable is buying whatever's cheap or throwing together a "diet" of table scraps. When choosing a diet for your Greyhound, there's no getting around the facts that quality counts and dogs eat only what appeals to them. You must also factor in what you have time to do and are comfortable doing.

The bottom line is that there's not just one good diet for your dog. All Greyhound owners I know are dedicated to their dogs' health and well-being. Yet some feed an entirely commercial diet, some home cook for their dogs, and others feed raw. Many combine two or all three of these options. I have had many dogs live long and healthy lives on commercial food. But today I feed my Greyhounds a combination of good-quality kibble formulated to meet a Greyhound's needs and Dr. Michael W. Fox's Homemade Natural Dietary Supplement for Dogs—in which he offers many choices. (See sidebar "Ask the Expert.")

Commercial Foods

With pet foods now a multi-billion-dollar industry in the United States, the number of commercial dog foods to choose from is exploding. Many brands provide the balanced nutrition dogs need without our having to cook for them. Wherever you decide to purchase your dog's food, make certain that the brand meets his nutritional needs. When purchasing dog food, don't forget to check the expiration date and make sure that there are no tears in dry-food bags or dents in cans.

Not all Greyhounds will do well on any particular food, so you may have to experiment before you find a brand or brands that your dog will both thrive on and enjoy. Health issues such as intestinal problems or persistent itching call for a change in food.

Dry Food

A high-quality dry dog food, or kibble, costs less and is more convenient than semi-moist and canned foods. It also promotes dental health by scraping tartar from the teeth while being chewed. Another bonus is that dogs fed high-quality kibble have smaller and firmer stools. But not all dogs like dry food, even moistened with water. Your world-class chowhound might be thrilled to

A high-quality dry dog food, or kibble, costs less and is more convenient than semi-moist and canned foods.

have plain kibble meal after meal, but a Greyhound with a discerning palate may look and sniff at his bowl, then walk dejectedly away to his bed. Some people foods you might add in small quantities to kibble, as flavor enhancements, include fish (try sardines), poultry, beef, vegetables (but not onions or garlic), well-cooked brown rice or oatmeal, unflavored nonfat yogurt, and low- or nonfat cottage cheese. (Don't add milk, though, as most dogs don't tolerate it well.) You can also mix in some good-quality canned food. Of course, adding water and soft food to kibble reduces its tartar-scraping benefit, but you were going to brush your Greyhound's teeth anyway.

A good dry food for the Greyhound who exercises daily but isn't involved in high-energy sports would have 22 to 27 percent protein, 10 to 15 percent fat, and 5 percent fiber. To maintain quality and flavor, transfer kibble from the bag it comes in to an airtight container, and wash the container before refilling it. This will prevent residual fat in the container from becoming rancid and contaminating the next bag of kibble you pour in.

Semi-Moist Food

Semi-moist dog food contains up to 40 percent water and really isn't a good value or a good choice for your Greyhound. He may like the soft, kibble-like chunks, but they'll stick to his teeth and undermine your efforts toward dental health—a major concern when it comes to Greyhounds. (See sidebar "Ask the Expert" in Chapter 5.) Most brands of semi-moist dog food contain dyes as well as preservatives that may include significant amounts of sugar. If you do choose to buy semi-moist food, consider purchasing a brand with organic ingredients.

Canned Food

Canned dog food doesn't deliver as much nutrition as kibble, because 75 percent or more of what's in the can is water. If the can is labeled "stew" or "with gravy," it may have a whopping 88 percent of water. Premium brands have better ingredients, so if you're going to mix canned food in with the dry, buy premium. Your vet may recommend canned food if your dog has a poor appetite because of illness or old age. Keep canned food refrigerated after

Your vet may recommend canned food if your dog has a poor appetite due to illness or old age.

FEEDING THE SENIOR GREYHOUND

If your older Greyhound's activity level has decreased significantly, you may have to curb calories. But with senior Greyhounds, there's usually more need to keep weight on than to take it off. Just as the nonracing Greyhound shouldn't be fed a high-protein diet, older Greyhounds should not be fed a low-protein "senior" diet. If your Greyhound eats commercial food, stay with the "adult" blend, as too little protein can cause muscle wasting and weight loss. Among the foods that may tempt an older dog to eat more are green tripe (not considered tasty by many humans, but what do we know?) and powdered liver, which should be used sparingly. Some dogs who are bored by kibble in a bowl find it tasty when given as treats. Be creative!

opening, and discard it if it's not used up by the time designated on the can—usually two days.

Noncommercial Foods

Some people decide against feeding their dog commercial foods and instead feed a homemade diet. In creating a noncommercial diet for your Greyhound, you have a choice between feeding him cooked or raw food. Either will allow you to control the ingredients and provide excellent quality, but there are disadvantages as well as advantages to both.

Home-Cooked Diet

A home-cooked diet is lip-licking delicious to most dogs, and many people who cook for their dog see improvement in his coat, weight, and vitality. But it takes time and energy—not to mention

research—to successfully feed a dog home-cooked meals. (Save time by cooking large batches and freezing the food in daily portions.) Of great importance is knowing what's safe and what isn't. Onions and garlic contain compounds that can damage a dog's red blood cells and cause anemia. (Garlic is less toxic than onions, hence the tiny amounts of garlic used in some dog foods for flavoring.) Large amounts of liver can cause vitamin A toxicity, affecting both muscles and bones. Dogs share our love of sweet foods, but like us they are prone to obesity and dental problems from eating sugary foods. Cooked bones of any kind can splinter and are very dangerous. There are many books and websites on the subject of home-cooked canine diets, and your vet can help you decide what's best for your dog.

Raw Diet

The bones and raw food diet ("BARF" for short)—consisting mostly of vegetables and meat, including bones—is considered dangerous by many people, but others consider the BARF diet to be superior nutrition. As with a home-cooked diet, you must do research and consult your vet to get BARF right. For instance, some foods that are safe for dogs when cooked are unsafe raw. Frequent feedings of raw fish can result in a thiamine (vitamin B1) deficiency and cause seizures. Raw eggs contain an enzyme that decreases absorption of biotin (vitamin H, or B7) and may cause problems of the skin and coat; worse, they may contain salmonella. Care in handling the raw foods, cleaning the utensils you use, and sanitizing work spaces is essential for your family's health. Feeding raw can also be time consuming and messy. But the fruits of your labor—as attested to by many Greyhound owners—include cleaner teeth, firmer stools, healthier skin and coat, and fewer allergies. Personally, I'll never know. The one time I offered each of my Greyhounds the meaty half of a raw chicken wing, Earl swallowed his whole and I nearly fainted.

Supplements

Giving dogs supplements is a controversial topic and one you should research and discuss with your veterinarian before administering them. If your Greyhound

A well-balanced diet will help keep your dog happy and healthy.

eats a high-quality diet, he probably doesn't need supplements. However, some medical conditions can be helped by supplements. Omega-3 and omega-6 fatty acids are important for allergic dogs, for example, but if the dog's diet provides plenty of omega-6 fatty acids, your veterinarian may prescribe only the omega-3s. Omega-3 fatty acids can also help reduce inflammation in arthritic dogs.

There are digestive enzymes marketed for dogs that when given daily will reduce the incidence of flatulence. Not all

Greys are gassy, but enough are for the phenomenon to be called Greyhound Gas. Other remedies to try for dogs who can clear a room include eliminating soy from the diet and giving a daily dollop of plain nonfat yogurt.

Be aware that human supplements may have ingredients your dog doesn't need (he manufactures his own vitamin C, which we don't do) and ingredients that may harm him. Too much iron can damage the lining of his digestive system and is toxic to the liver and kidneys.

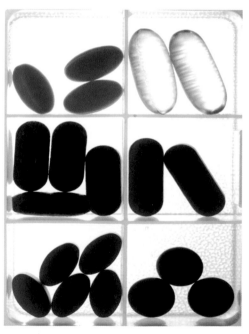

Check with your vet before administering supplements to your dog.

My dogs get a daily softgel of omega-3s and one half of a senior multivitamin for humans that does not have iron—crushed and mixed in the first meal of the day.

Treats

Treats add to a dog's love of life and are an essential tool for training. Choose healthy treats for your Greyhound, and have him earn them by obeying a command: *come*, *sit* (if he's comfortable sitting), *down*, etc. By doing this, with each treat you'll reaffirm that you're in charge, reinforce training, contribute to his overall health, and make him happy. Treats don't have to be big, expensive, fattening, or fancy—just healthful. My dogs sit for kibble. But giving them peanut butter wrapped in spinach is a treat for me too.

Reading Food Labels

Pet food labels serve to tell consumers what's in the food and get them to buy it. By law, five pieces of information must be on the label: guaranteed analysis (including a "life stage" claim), nutritional adequacy statement, ingredients, feeding guidelines, and the manufacturer's name and address. Many words and phrases on labels have no standard definition or regulatory meaning and thus are of no significance. These include "senior," "premium," "natural," "improves doggy breath," and "recommended by veterinarians." The words "beef dog

DR. MICHAEL W. FOX'S
HOMEMADE NATURAL DIETARY SUPPLEMENT FOR DOGS

INGREDIENTS

2 cups uncooked whole grain rice
  (or barley, rolled oats, or pasta
  noodles)
  pinch of salt
1 cup raw, grated carrots, sweet
  potato, or yam (mix well into the
  stew while it is still very hot)
1 T. safflower oil or flaxseed oil (if
  using flaxseed oil, add it to the
  cooked food after it has cooled
  down to room temperature)
1 T. cider vinegar
1 t. brewer's yeast
1 t. calcium carbonate, citrate, or
  lactate
1 t. dried kelp
1 lb. (0.5 kg) lean hamburger, ground
  lamb, mutton, or one whole
  chicken or half of a small turkey

DIRECTIONS

Combine all ingredients as directed. Add water to cover ingredients, simmer, stir, and add more water as needed until cooked. (Debone chicken parts and do not feed cooked bones because they can splinter and cause internal injury.) The recipe should be thick to be molded into patties. (Add oat bran or meal to help thicken.) Serve 1 cup of this recipe for a 30-pound (13.5 kg) dog with the rest of his rations, freeze the rest into patties, and store in the freezer. Serve thawed or frozen to gnaw on outdoors in hot weather.

Also give the dog a daily multivitamin and multi-mineral supplement, such as Pfizer's Pet-Tabs or a good-quality human "one-a-day" supplement equivalent, crushed up in the food, calculating one-half of the human daily dose for a 50-pound (22.5-kg) dog. (But always check with your veterinarian on whether feeding this kind of supplement is appropriate for your individual dog.)

For variation on the above recipe, you can use cottage cheese plus well-cooked lentils, chickpeas (garbanzo beans), lima beans, or other pulses, or a dozen eggs as meat alternatives. Lightly cooked raw calf or beef liver and heart and kidneys are good sources of animal protein and other essential nutrients. All pet food ingredients, ideally, should be organically certified. (Note: Some dogs are allergic or hypersensitive to some foods, especially soy, beef, eggs, wheat, and dairy products.).

NOTE: For dogs weighing less than 30 pounds (13.5 kg) and for overweight and less active dogs, use 1 cup of uncooked rice in the recipe. The recipe can also be fed as a complete meal rather than a supplement. Mix increasing amounts of your dog's new food with decreasing amounts of the old food over a seven-day period to enable adaptation and prevent possible digestive upset. It's advisable to vary the basic ingredients to provide variety and prevent possible nutritional imbalances. Monitor the dog's body condition so as to prevent over- or underfeeding—based on the average dog consuming 1 cup of the food twice daily per 30 pounds (13.5 kg) of body weight.

NOTE: Different dogs have different nutritional needs according to age, temperament, amount of physical activity, and health status. Large dogs require less food per 1 pound (0.5 kg) of body weight, so adjust according to appetite and weight gain.

Used by permission of Dr. Michael W. Fox, a syndicated columnist and member of the Royal College of Veterinary Surgeons.

To keep your Greyhound at a healthy weight, feed him a nutritious diet and exercise him regularly.

food" or "chicken for dogs" mean that the product contains at least 70 percent of beef or chicken. The percentage of beef or chicken drops to a minimum of 25 percent when "platter" or "dinner" is part of the description, and the word "formula," as in "dog formula with beef," brings the minimum percentage to 3 percent. Add the word "flavor," as in "chicken flavored," and the meat in the product is virtually nil. Some words, such as "animal by-products," put people off a particular food. But the protein quality of by-products—which may contain heads, feet, viscera, and other body parts that don't stimulate most people's appetite—is sometimes better than protein from muscle meat.

There's much to be learned about pet food labels, and it can be found at www.fda.gov/cvm, the website of the U.S. Food and Drug Administration's (FDA) Center for Veterinary Medicine.

Changing Foods

If your Greyhound comes from an adoption group or reputable breeder, you can find out what his diet consisted of and keep it the same while he adjusts to his new surroundings. Change—even happy change—is stressful to all beings. If your Grey has just retired from racing, the transition from his racing diet to kibble may cause loose stools. Even without an abrupt change in diet, his stools may be loose at first. This isn't cause for concern. But if he has diarrhea and it lasts more than 24 hours, call your veterinarian.

Any time a dog's diet is altered, it should be done gradually to prevent stomach upset. On the first two days, your Greyhound's meals should consist of 3/4 of his old food and 1/4 of the new food. The next two days the old food and new food may be divided evenly. On days five and six, go to 1/4 old food and 3/4 new food. By day seven, your Grey should be well enough adjusted to his new food for the old food to be retired.

Should your dog suddenly lose interest in the kibble he greatly enjoyed before or have loose stools where before they were firm, the formula in his kibble may have changed. The manufacturer does not have to announce this on the package. When one of my Greyhounds turned her back on her food bowl and the other had an upset stomach, I learned that the brand I had carefully chosen and had been successful with for several years had been altered. The company announced the change on its website but not on the packaging.

Feeding Schedules

The choices of when to feed your Greyhound include "free feeding," making food accessible at all times and letting him eat as much as he wants, and scheduled feeding, which is just as it sounds—making food available only at scheduled times. Free feeding is rarely recommended, and it does seem vital that we regulate how much and at what time our Greyhounds eat. Many Greys would stuff themselves to the point of indigestion, or worse, if free fed. (Even pigs at a trough are not free fed; it's all monitored.) It's also important to monitor what your Greyhound does after eating. This is a good time for a long snooze. You may take him outside to eliminate, but don't let him run and don't take him on a walk, not even a slow walk, as the side-to-side swaying of his stomach while walking could invite trouble.

Food and Safety

Many foods and other substances that people enjoy are dangerous for dogs. Sugary foods can lead to dental problems and obesity, so why give them to a dog when there's a wealth of healthy treats for him to enjoy? And never give your dog anything with the sugar substitute xylitol in it. Found in products ranging from sugar-free chewing gum to baked goods, xylitol is toxic to dogs and can cause liver failure. If you think that your dog may have eaten

Check It Out

FEEDING CHECKLIST

✓ Know your food basics.
✓ Read the ingredients on commercial dog food.
✓ Consider the types of commercial food.
✓ Weigh the pluses and minuses of commercial, home-cooked, and raw diets.
✓ With the help of your vet, choose whether to give supplements.

✓ Change foods gradually to prevent stomach upset.
✓ Make food safety a priority—and when in doubt, don't feed that item.
✓ Teach good table manners.
✓ Prevent obesity by feeding your dog a nutritious diet and encouraging sufficient exercise.

something containing xylitol, call your vet. A good rule to live by is that if you don't know for certain that something is safe for your Greyhound to eat, find out before allowing him to have it.

Here's a short list of what isn't safe. The caffeine in chocolate, coffee, and tea can affect the heart and nervous system. Grapes and raisins may damage the kidneys. Macadamia nuts have an unknown toxin that can harm muscles and the digestive and nervous systems. The skin and flesh of an apple are safe, but the seeds have cyanide in them. Mushrooms—whether from your refrigerator or the yard—are not for dogs. Greyhounds shouldn't have access to cat food; it's too high in protein for them. Alcohol, as you can imagine, could cause death. The list goes on, so when in doubt, find out.

Obesity

Obesity is rampant among dogs and does them nothing but harm. Disorders that ensue from overeating make a dog's life uncomfortable while shortening it. Our dogs become fat only if we feed them too much, so let's not do it. A retired racer should stay within 5 pounds (2.5 kg) of his racing weight, and a rule of thumb for any Greyhound is that you should see a slight indentation between his last three ribs and easily be able to feel the ribs with your hands.

Table Manners

Greyhounds love to eat; even the picky eaters do, except that they want to order from a menu. But Greyhounds typically don't go into a frenzy at chow time. This is fortunate because frenzies are stressful, and stress before eating is unhealthful.

Some people teach their dogs to sit while waiting to eat, but many Greyhounds find sitting uncomfortable, so standing calmly should be enough. Couch potatoes that Greyhounds are, your dog might even remain lying down until you put the bowl on the floor.

If you have more than one dog, each should have his own feeding station and be fed in the order that he came into your home. This assures the dog who joined your family first that he's still number one and prevents jealousy.

Whether you're preparing a meal for your dog or for yourself, begging should never be rewarded. And don't feed your Greyhound from the table or when you're snacking in front of the television, not even a crumb. If you do, he won't forget it and won't believe your earnest proclamations that it's not going to happen again. It's fine for him to lie near you while you eat, perhaps with a chew toy, like a Nylabone, to take his mind off what you're chewing. If you eat breakfast at home, have yours before he has his. He may be the master of your heart, but you outrank him.

As dog owners, we are very fortunate to know so much more about a dog's nutritional needs than was known only a few years ago. We have options, good ones, in choosing what to feed our canine family members. And because we do, pet food manufacturers that want to stay in business and really do care about pet health are offering us better formulas and better quality.

Chapter
5

Grooming
Your Greyhound

When it comes to grooming, Greyhounds are low maintenance. They are light shedders with a short single coat, so removal of loose hair is a breeze. The daily grooming of your Greyhound should take little time and be pleasant for you both. You'll spend a couple of minutes brushing his coat and a few more brushing his teeth. Nail trimming may be done once or twice a week or even every other week—depending on how fast his nails grow. Bathing is seldom required. But don't skip the daily coat brushing and teeth brushing. They are among the "ties that bind" for you and your dog, and they help *you* to help *him* stay healthy.

Grooming as a Health Check

Grooming your Greyhound every day gives you the opportunity to detect possible health problems early on, not after they've become advanced. In short time you'll have come to know every part of his body, so you'll know when there's a change anywhere. Eye, ear, or skin problems; tumors; inflammation of the gums—none of these will elude you. Doctors tell us to get to know our own bodies and be alert for any changes. We should do no less for our dogs.

When grooming your Greyhound, be alert for:

- lumps, cuts, or sores on any part of the body
- sensitivity to touch anywhere on the body
- runny or excessive discharge from the eyes, ears, or nose
- bad odor from the mouth or ears
- hot and dry nose
- red or irritated-looking eyes
- unexplained hair loss
- signs of parasites or other skin problems

Puppy Love

GROOMING A PUPPY

If your new Greyhound is a puppy, you will want to socialize him to grooming right away. As with anything else you teach your dog, the grooming session should be kept short. And above all, it should be fun—an easy, gentle game he's learning in which he gets treated for staying still while you touch his ears, tail, and feet. After you've touched one foot for a few seconds, treat him. When you touch another foot, give him another treat. Your hands and the grooming brush should always be gentle on him, so there's nothing for him to fear.

Grooming Supplies

Here is a short list of supplies that will help keep your Greyhound well groomed:

- cotton balls or ear wipes
- dog conditioner (cream rinse formula)
- dog shampoo (tear-free)
- dog toothbrush and toothpaste
- ear-cleaning solution
- emery board
- flea comb
- nail clippers or grinder (plug-in or cordless)
- oil-free dry skin spray (if needed)
- shedding blade (for Greys with a thicker coat)

- soft brush or hound glove
- styptic powder, flour, or cornstarch

You may be wondering whether you need a grooming table for your Greyhound, and the answer is no, you won't need one to groom him at home. He's tall enough to be groomed standing on the floor, and if given his druthers, he would prefer it this way. Besides, grooming him isn't a timely task. If you show your Greyhound, before entering the ring he will have his whiskers trimmed, as well as any stray hairs, and tufts of hair in his ears will be shaved. But this is usually done with the dog standing on the floor, unless the handler wants to chalk some spots, which is easier to do on a grooming table. Whiskers trimmed? Chalk? What price beauty!

Coat and Skin Care

All dogs gain confidence in themselves and their people by having a schedule. Like you, your Greyhound will appreciate knowing what time of day his hair gets brushed and when his teeth will be cleaned.

Brushing

Brushing your Greyhound removes loose hair and helps distribute the natural oils that keep his coat shiny. If you begin a routine of brushing your dog at the same time every day, it will become a ritual he'll look forward to, so try not to miss a day.

A tear-free dog shampoo will help keep your Greyhound's coat looking its best.

How to Brush the Coat

Using a soft brush or hound glove, gently brush over the top of his head and down his back, sides, chest, neck, legs, and tail. Always brush in the direction his coat grows, and brush his belly only if he grows hair there. It's common for Greyhound tummies to be sparsely coated or almost hairless, requiring only gentle and affectionate rubbing, not brushing.

Some Greyhounds shed more than others or are seasonal shedders who "blow" their coats twice a year. If yours is one of those types, you might want to purchase a shedding blade. Not necessary but useful, the shedding blade is looped for use on smaller areas such as the chest, shoulders, upper arms, sides of the thighs, and the tail. It can be opened for use on wider areas such as the dog's back and sides. Always be gentle when using the shedding blade; you don't have to push hard as you glide it over your dog's coat.

Bathing

Because Greyhounds have little oil in their skin, they don't need frequent baths. In fact, too much bathing can irritate their skin. It's usually recommended that unless your Greyhound gets dirty playing in the yard or has a flea problem, a bath once or twice a year is sufficient. Some people prefer more frequent bathing, while others feel strongly that a dog who is brushed every day doesn't need a bath unless he becomes soiled. I go with the once or twice a year theory, but there's no right or wrong here. When you bathe your Greyhound, have a second person (not a young child) with you if possible. Your helper can keep the dog from jumping out of the bathtub or shower stall if he gets nervous or gently hold him if he gets wobbly.

Use a tearless puppy shampoo, a gentle conditioning shampoo, or any good doggy shampoo followed by a doggy conditioner. Never use shampoo made for

A bath once or twice a year is usually sufficient for a Greyhound.

Greyhounds are low maintenance when it comes to grooming—and it doesn't take much effort to keep them looking great.

humans, not even a baby shampoo, as it will irritate your dog's skin.

How to Bathe the Coat

Put a bath mat or bath towel on the bottom of the tub or shower before your dog gets in, to make him feel more secure. Use only lukewarm to medium-warm water. This is because Greyhounds have too little fat to regulate their body temperature to hot or cold water. Unless you use a tearless shampoo, don't

shampoo his face; just wipe it. And don't get water in his ears. (You may try putting a dry cotton ball in each ear, but he'll probably shake them out.) After shampooing, make sure to rinse him all over, then use a soft towel to dry him gently but thoroughly. One more *very* important thing: Throughout the entire bathing process, talk cheerfully to your boy and lavish praise on him.

If your dog has dry skin, which usually happens in winter, you can try bathing him with a shampoo that has oatmeal as a main ingredient. This is soothing and provides moisture. You might also try rubbing or spraying on your dog's coat an oil-free humectant, a substance that helps retain moisture. Your veterinarian may also recommend adding a fatty acid supplement to his diet.

Your Greyhound may show food stains at the sides of his mouth after eating, especially if he's light colored. Gently clean the area with a wet washcloth, sponge, or paper towels.

Preventing Sunburn

Greyhounds tend to be sun worshippers. They'll lie in the sunniest part of the yard, and indoors they'll follow sunlight streaking through the windows. Sunlight is healthy for our dogs and for us because it helps produce vitamin D. But too much ultraviolet (UV) radiation from the sun causes sunburn, or solar dermatitis, in dogs, which can lead to severe skin problems, including cancer. Sunburn is most common in light-colored and shorthaired dogs, so protect your Grey from getting too much sun by applying a sunscreen when necessary. Use it on his ear tips, nose (but not near his eyes), rump (if bald or partly bald), and abdomen. After applying the sunscreen, keep him distracted for a while so that he won't lick it off his belly. Pet stores sell sunscreen made for dogs, but one formulated for babies works just as well and is safe for your dog. Bear in mind that UV radiation can pass through windows and that a dark-haired Greyhound—while not as susceptible to skin cancer—overheats quickly, and this too is dangerous.

Nail Care

Retired racing Greyhounds are used to having their feet handled, but like most other dogs they don't relish having their nails trimmed. Nail trimming is an essential part of grooming, though, and

EXCITEMENT SHEDDING

Some Greyhounds shed when they're excited. A likely time for this to happen is when you and your dog are at a Greyhound meet and greet event, and you've just told a potential adopter that Greyhounds aren't heavy shedders. The person starts petting your dog, who loves nothing more than having strangers pet him, and he shows his joy by releasing copious amounts of hair that stick to the person's hand. There may also be dandruff on your dog's back, which he didn't have before the meet and greet and will not have after it. This happened every time I took my dark brindle boy, Earl, to a meet and greet. Show Greyhounds do it too—at dog shows. Their handlers control excitement shedding and dandruff by spraying Listerine on the dog, a quick and safe method that also makes him smell extra nice. (In fact, many people who are prone to dandruff use Listerine on themselves.) But for meet and greets, I prefer not to use it. If a stranger pets my dog and the excitement leads to a little shedding and dandruff, it creates an opportunity to tell the stranger about Greyhounds and how much they love socializing and being petted. Every time we talk to people interested in our dogs, we plant the seed for more retired racers to be adopted.

if you can hear your dog's nails clicking against the floor, it's time to trim them. Use a guillotine-style nail clipper (they're shaped like pliers) or a grinding tool. Guillotine-style clippers—which can't slip and injure your dog, as human nail clippers can—are available at any pet supply store, as are grinding tools.

Nail trimming really isn't hard to do, but if you're not sure you want to try it, it can be done at your veterinarian clinic or a dog grooming salon. To trim your dog's nails at home, it's best to have another adult there to help keep him still and calm and to cheerfully administer very small treats during the clipping or grinding process.

The object of nail trimming is to keep the nails at a comfortable, healthy length. Be wary of cutting or grinding too close to the quick of the nail. If your dog has white nails, it will be easier to see where the quick—which is pink—begins. On black nails, the quick isn't visible. Go slowly. Trim a little bit at a time. It's better to trim more often than to accidentally injure your dog by trying to do too much at once.

How to Trim the Nails

Your dog may be standing or lying on his side, whichever he's comfortable with. If he's standing, bend each foot backward so that you can see the underside of the nail. Hold his paw firmly but without squeezing, and cut just the tip of the nail. This is so that you won't cut the quick, which supplies blood to the nail. If his nails are white, you'll see the quick. It's a pink line in the middle of the nail that extends almost to the nail's end. If your dog's nails are dark, clip just the hooked end of the nail. An electric or battery-operated grinder is especially good for trimming dark nails that don't show the quick, and most people find a grinder easier to use. I prefer a plug-in grinder because it's more powerful, and I don't have to worry that the battery will die in the middle of a trimming session. A battery-operated grinder, however, has the advantage of greater mobility.

If the noise frightens your dog, there are ways to distract him. One is to smear a little peanut butter on the roof of his mouth. Or you can smear peanut butter on the refrigerator door for him to lick while you work. My favorite method is to have the dog lie on a dog bed with his head on my lap. While my husband operates the grinder, I feed a very small treat as each nail is trimmed. A family friend whom your dog adores can do this with you. Just make sure that you have enough treats.

However you trim your Greyhound's nails, keep styptic powder (or flour or cornstarch) on hand to stanch the bleeding if you accidentally cut into the quick. Dip the nail into the styptic powder and apply pressure for a few minutes and the bleeding will stop. You may murmur to your dog that you're sorry, but don't act upset or he'll think something really bad happened to him. After all of his nails are trimmed, you can use an emery board to smooth rough edges, if necessary.

After your Greyhound's nails are trimmed, you can use an emery board to smooth rough edges.

Because of his short, thin hair and little body fat, your Greyhound needs outerwear to protect him from the elements.

By trimming your dog's nails frequently, you'll cause the quicks to recede. Then you can keep his nails a bit shorter.

Dewclaws

If your dog still has his dewclaws, they too will need trimming. Dewclaws are the nails about a third of the way up the forelegs in what are known as the vestigial toes. These nonweight-bearing extra toes are normal in many species. Show Greyhounds have their dewclaws removed when they're a few days old.

Many racing Greyhounds also have their dewclaws removed, but removing them isn't required, so some retired racers have them and some don't. Dewclaws don't touch the ground and have no real purpose, except to an imaginative fellow like my Bruce, who thinks that his dewclaws are built-in chew toys.

Ear Care

If your dog is sensitive to having his ears handled, it could be that someone wasn't gentle when checking his tattoos before

GROOMING CHECKLIST

✓ Brush the coat daily.
✓ Bathe once or twice a year or as necessary.

✓ Inspect the eyes and ears daily.
✓ Trim the nails weekly or biweekly, as necessary.
✓ Brush the teeth daily.

a race. He'll get over this sensitivity after experiencing your light touch on his ears, and in short time he will even enjoy a gentle ear massage. Talk to him when you touch his ears. Tell him how soft they are—just made for stroking. He'll come around in time.

How to Care for the Ears

After your dog has become accustomed to having his ears handled, check them once a week and clean them if necessary. Accumulated earwax can cause infection, but it's easy to clean. Moisten a cotton ball or a piece of cloth wrapped around your index finger with ear cleanser that you purchase at a pet shop. Special ear wipes can also be found at pet stores and veterinary clinics. Do *not* use cotton swabs for cleaning your dog's ears or insert your finger any deeper into the ear than it comfortably fits and you can see. This could injure the eardrum or canal.

If your Greyhound shakes his head violently or repeatedly scratches an ear and the problem persists, he may have an ear infection or, less likely, ear mites (mostly seen in cats, not dogs). A bad smell, black crust, or discharge from the ear also signals trouble. Don't try to treat an ear problem yourself. See your vet.

Eye Care

Looking into your Greyhound's eyes and seeing his trust in you is one of the sweetest pleasures of having him in your family.

How to Care for the Eyes

On a regular basis, look carefully at his eyes to see whether anything's amiss there. Signs of a potentially serious eye problem include redness, a thick mucus discharge, squinting, and itchiness (evidenced by his rubbing the affected eye). A bit of mucus in the corners of your dog's eyes is normal, but letting it build up creates a breeding ground for bacteria. When you see mucus, gently wipe it away with a moist washcloth or tissue.

Eye care for your Greyhound also includes protecting his eyes from injury.

Check your Greyhound's eyes regularly to ensure that they are clean and healthy.

Soap and chemicals can seriously damage eye tissues as, of course, can foreign objects. When your Grey rides in a vehicle, don't let him stick his head or even his muzzle out the window. The possibility of permanent injury from a bug or debris hitting him in the eye isn't worth the risk.

Dental Care

Greyhounds form tartar quickly, so faithfully brushing your Grey's teeth (daily is ideal) is essential to keeping him from having dental problems. Fortunately, before being adopted retired racers have their teeth professionally cleaned while under anesthesia for spaying or neutering. So whether your new family member is a puppy with healthy young teeth or an adult dog, you have a head start in preventing future dental problems. Home care of your dog's teeth and cleaning by a veterinarian when necessary are vitally important because periodontal disease can ultimately lead to diseases of the heart, liver, and kidneys. At the very least, neglecting your dog's teeth will result in gingivitis (inflammation of the gums) and tooth loss. This happens because food particles that stick to the dog's gum

CLEAN AS A HOUND'S TOOTH

—Rodger Barr, DVM

If given the opportunity to alter this nearly perfect breed of dog, the Greyhound, I would give this fabulous breed a perfect set of teeth.

The reality is that Greyhounds are prone to a lifetime of dental disease. There are many hypotheses to explain the huge amount of painful, decaying plaque that these mouths harbor. Suffice it to say that the combination of limited gnawing and chewing opportunities combined with a high-quality but stew-like diet lends itself well to plaque formation at a very early age. Once the plaque has a chance to take hold, it can result in gum recession and concomitant gingivitis, infection, and ultimately the untimely loss of teeth—often a large number of teeth.

Assuming that when your newly adopted family member arrives his oral cavity has been properly managed, the burden of care now lies with you. If you or your pet is reluctant to brush or be brushed, the inevitable will be the need for regular dental prophylaxis, expensive veterinary bills, anesthesia risks, and the loss of nonreplaceable teeth. All of this is preventable with unwavering commitment to daily brushing. Twice daily is twice as good. Once a week is useless. Twice weekly is half as useless. A commonly used adage by your own dentist states: "Only brush the teeth you want to keep." This is true for Greyhounds also. Make dental care a routine. Do it at the same time every day, and do it without fail. This is a very small price to pay for unconditional love, don't you think?

line and remain there harbor bacteria that soon form plaque, a raised patch that in turn becomes an incrustation on the gums and teeth, called tartar. It's this incrustation—or calculus—that causes gingivitis.

Persistent bad breath in a dog isn't always caused by periodontal disease, but it needs looking into. Other symptoms of periodontal disease include red or swollen gums, a yellow or brown crust near the gum line, sensitivity to touch, and of course, loose or missing teeth. The dog may also resist eating because it hurts to chew.

How to Care for the Teeth

Use a doggy toothbrush (it looks like yours but has a longer handle and is softer) or a "finger brush" that fits over your finger. Buy doggy toothpaste because dogs don't spit, and human toothpaste can make your dog sick. Besides, doggy toothpaste comes in yummy flavors, with "chicken flavor" probably the best loved by Greyhounds. Start slowly, brushing the outer surfaces of the teeth in an up-and-down motion. You don't have to brush the backs of the teeth, as your dog takes care of that with the movement of his tongue.

Consider using an oral hygiene spray made for dogs, which your veterinarian clinic probably carries. When used as directed, the spray is effective in reducing

Your Greyhound's teeth should be brushed every day.

bacteria that lead to gingivitis but does not take the place of brushing your dog's teeth. Hard dog biscuits given as snacks and chew toys used under supervision are also helpful—but they too will not take the place of daily brushing.

Grooming your Greyhound is a brief and gentle process that will quickly fit into your daily routine. Your dog will know that you care, and you may give yourself an "A" for a job well done.

Chapter
6

Training
Your Greyhound

I'm convinced that a trained dog is a happy dog and that an untrained dog is as unhappy as a child who hasn't been taught good manners and is often out of control. Because the trained dog knows what he should and should not do, he's spared the frustration of uncertainty and the unpleasantness of frequent reprimands. He has confidence in himself, enjoys a deeper bond with his family, and is a pleasure to be with both indoors and out.

Train From the Beginning

Training begins when you bring your Greyhound home and walk him in the yard on leash before taking him indoors—also on leash. Everything he encounters—whether he's a puppy or a retired racer—is new to him, and he has to be taught how to respond to it all. You do this with positive training, which means rewarding him every time he does something right, even if you didn't ask him to do it. If you don't want him to lift his leg on the garden bench, steer him to where you would like him to urinate and praise him when he does. If he walks nicely at your side, praise him for this too. He's feeling a little stressed and needs to know that he's a good boy. He also needs consistency—firm rules that don't change and everyone in his family using the same words and methods to train him.

Be Positive

Your "tools" for positive training are treats, praise, and petting. Don't use your hands to punish, only to praise. If your Greyhound doesn't obey a command, he doesn't get rewarded—but he doesn't get scolded, either. Every training session should be short, easy, and fun.

What treats to use in training depend on where your Greyhound stands on the chowhound scale. If he's easy to thrill, his regular kibble—nutritious and kind to teeth and gums—will suffice. But for the Greyhound gourmet, you'll need to up the ante. Tiny bites of dog biscuits, pieces of hot dog (zap them in the microwave to make them less greasy), cheese, cereal, fruits (but not raisins or grapes, which are toxic to dogs), and raw carrots or green beans are enjoyed by most dogs. Once in a while, end a training session by letting your dog win the jackpot—a small handful of treats.

Bite-sized treats are a good training reward.

TIPS ON TRAINING YOUR GREYHOUND

—Lee Livingood, Certified Dog Behavior Consultant, International
Association of Animal Behavior Consultants (IAABC)

1. Keep it simple and make it fun. Draw on your dog's natural abilities and instincts; think about what he loves and what he was bred to do.

2. Use life rewards—whatever he wants now (a walk, a ride, a chance to greet another dog) is a life reward.

3. Be silly. Act up or calm down depending on your dog's personality.

4. Minimize repetition. (Do a command two or three times, then change the picture or work on something completely different.)

5. Work for only a few minutes at a time.

6. Learning is stressful. Stop before your dog gets stressed.

7. Let him know when he's released to do something else, and let him know when a training session is over.

8. Always leave him wanting more.

Be Consistent

While training your dog and for the rest of his life, try not to vary the way you communicate with him. For commands, use the same words and hand signals. "Max, come" and "Here, Max" may be synonymous to you, but to your dog they aren't. Also avoid using your dog's name in combination with "No," or "Wrong," as his name shouldn't be said in a scolding tone. But do use it to begin an action command. When you say "Max, sit" or "Max, come," his name alerts him that he's to begin an action. For a command that tells him to remain still, leave off his name. "Stay," for example, requires no action and does not begin with his name.

Training is forever. Long after your Greyhound has learned to sit on command, he will associate sitting with being rewarded. So if he suddenly sits and looks up at you expectantly, reward him with praise and petting. He loves your voice and the touch of your hand.

Socialization

Socialization is introducing a dog to a variety of situations so that he'll be comfortable with the world around him. A dog who doesn't learn early that the world

Puppies must be taken outside to eliminate after eating, playing, or waking from sleep.

is a friendly place may grow up anxious and develop fear-related aggression. Puppies first socialize with their "birth family" (mama dog and littermates) and their breeder's family and friends. Racing Greyhounds socialize with many of their kind as well as trainers and handlers and possibly kids. But your dog is in a new environment and needs new socialization, especially to children (even if you don't have any) and to other pets.

How to Socialize Your Greyhound to Children

All dogs should be socialized to children, but no dog should be subjected to rough play or angry behavior. The goal, then, is to socialize dogs to children and children to dogs. Rarely will a Greyhound bite anyone unless sorely provoked, and most Greys

enjoy being petted by children. But one incident of a child's climbing on your dog, pulling his ears or tail, or hitting or kicking him can make him fear all children. Teach your kids and their friends who visit not to rush up to any dog, to keep their hands away from a dog's face, to pet gently, and not to disturb a sleeping dog.

One way to socialize your dog to kids is to take him to Greyhound meet and greets held at pet supply stores. There he will likely meet children who have dogs and know how to interact with them. And the well-behaved children of your friends who visit your home can also help socialize your Greyhound to kids.

How to Socialize Your Greyhound to Other Pets

For racing Greyhounds, living with other

TRAIN PEOPLE TOO!

Greyhounds go down stairs quickly and really have no choice because of how they're built. Going upstairs, some Greys take one step at a time, while others seem to fly up. Caution children (and houseguests) to hug the wall and let the dog go up or down stairs first. Also, Greyhounds racing at full speed can stop on a dime and enjoy running straight to a person to do it. The experience can be frightening to someone visiting you, especially a young child or older person. For this reason, it's wise not to leave kids or guests alone in a fenced yard with your Greyhound off leash.

dogs is natural. But a Greyhound who hasn't grown up around small animals may think that they're prey and act accordingly. Your Greyhound should be tested for cat safety before you adopt him, but even if he is deemed low prey (not inclined to give chase), don't assume that it's safe to leave him alone with your cat. Use caution introducing any animal to another, and continue supervising them together long after you think they're compatible. A retired racer should wear a muzzle—which he's used to doing—when he's around a cat until you're certain that it's safe for him not to be muzzled. And even if your Greyhound and cat become best friends, don't trust your dog with someone else's cat.

Crate Training

As noted in Chapter 3, a crate is your dog's personal space, his den, a place where he knows that he's safe from harm. Only good things happen in his crate. He gets treats for going into his crate. On occasion he gets an incredibly wonderful treat in his crate. The bedding in his crate is kept clean and is as comfortable as he could wish. And his crate is *never* used to punish him. Only good dogs get to be crated.

There. Feel better? You really needn't feel guilty about crating your dog as long as he can stand up and turn around in the crate and isn't in it for an unreasonable length of time. Crating for longer than four hours at a time during the day isn't fair, and if he's crated during the day, he shouldn't be at night.

Crates have many uses: housetraining, keeping a dog quiet while he recuperates from surgery, keeping him from being underfoot when necessary, and in a multi-dog home, preventing one dog from eating another's meal. But to me the main function of crates is to keep my Greyhounds from tearing through the house and injuring themselves while I'm out.

BEDTIME

The best place for your new Greyhound to sleep is in your bedroom. He isn't used to being alone at night, and sleeping near you will make him feel secure. If he's not crated at night, baby gate the bedroom to keep him from roaming.

You will want an extra-large-sized crate for dogs weighing over 50 pounds (22.5 kg). It's best for a crate to have nothing in it except washable bedding. However, in cases of separation anxiety (see Chapter 7), leaving a durable Nylabone chew toy can be helpful. Also, it's safe to leave your dog crated with a durable rubber toy stuffed with peanut butter and then frozen—which will make the pleasurable job of eating the peanut butter take much longer. Leaving a safe and yummy chewy in the crate with your dog will help him focus on something other than your absence. And by the time he's through chewing, he may feel ready for a good long snooze, which is the kind of snoozing Greyhounds love to do.

How to Crate Train

Your Greyhound may instantly take to his crate—or not. Train him to "kennel" or "kennel up" by tossing a treat into the crate and praising him when he goes in to get it. In no time the word "kennel" should have him rushing to his crate before you toss the treat. But some dogs love their crates except when "kennel" means that Mom or Dad is going out. (Your dog does know you're leaving, even if you try to keep it secret.) If your dog won't kennel, don't repeat the command. Take him gently by the collar and walk him to his crate. When he goes in, treat him. He's a good boy.

In spite of treats and encouragement, the retired racer may feel that retirement means never having to be crated again. Still, with positive reinforcement, combined with your staying calm, he will come around. After all, he is very used to being crated, not only at the track but also in his adoption group's kennel or the foster home in which he was placed.

The first few times you crate your dog and leave, come back in a few minutes. Always be casual about leaving (no goodbyes are necessary) and just as casual on your return. Your being reunited should not be a big deal, as this may reinforce his feeling of anxiety on your leaving.

With two Greyhounds who resisted crating, I began by crating them and not leaving the house. Instead, I sat near the crate and read to them. After listening to me read the morning paper a few times, they didn't mind my leaving for a few minutes, and then a half hour, and then even longer intervals until they were used to being left for several hours. It's a good idea to have music on whenever you leave—even long after your dog has grown used to being crated.

Housetraining

A dog who isn't housetrained is as unhappy as the owner who has to clean up the messes (sometimes after stepping in them), so housetraining is the first order of the day whether your new dog

is a puppy or retired racer. If the latter, he's already used to scheduled bathroom outings from his life at the farm and track and at the Greyhound adoption group where he was placed in retirement. Your job will be easy.

How to Housetrain

Housetraining a puppy is about getting him outdoors to do his business before he does it indoors. You must simply assume that after eating, playing, or waking from sleep, your puppy needs to go. Take him to where you would like him to relieve himself, say "Go potty" (or whatever command you choose), and praise and treat him when he does. Greyhound

Training your dog makes him a pleasure to live with and helps keep him safe.

puppies have a fast metabolism, so what goes in may come out sooner than with other breeds. Be diligent, and realize that if he has an accident, it's your fault for not getting him outside in time.

To reinforce a newly retired racer's habit of eliminating only outdoors, be sure that he knows where the door to his bathroom is and take him outside through that door when he gets up in the morning, within a half hour after each meal, anytime you come home and uncrate him, and before bedtime. Don't give him the run of the house until you're confident that he's reliable, and feed him his last meal of the day at least four hours before bedtime. Always be fair. If you sleep in on weekends, your dog can't wait the extra hours to relieve himself.

There's a good chance that your Greyhound won't need the bathroom your first night together, but if he whines or is restless, leash him and take him outside. Don't play while you're out there, or you may "train" him that 3 a.m. is playtime. Quietly praise him for doing his business, and bring him back to bed.

Keep your Greyhound's bathroom pleasant and safe for him. Pick up feces each time he goes or at least daily. If your yard fills with snow in winter, you'll need to shovel a walking path and a "poop station" for his comfort. You can protect him from slipping on ice by using a pet-safe ice melt product.

Basic Obedience Commands

Your Greyhound can be taught many things. This section covers basic behaviors and describes how to teach them to make your dog a pleasure to live with and help keep him safe.

Always have treats handy when teaching a command, but don't try to train him when he's tired or hot. Except for teaching him to be a good walking partner, it's best to work indoors—on a carpeted surface for his comfort—to minimize distractions.

Come

Teaching your Greyhound to come to you on command will prevent countless instances of your having to chase after him in the house and in the yard—and chasing a Greyhound can be an exercise in futility. It could also save his life if he ever got loose. Even before you begin teaching *come*, reward him every time he comes to you. A treat, praise, or petting all say the same thing: *You're a good dog!*

How to Teach Come

1. With your dog on leash and treats in your hand, cheerfully say "Max, come" and *without repeating the command*, get him to come to you by any means. Be playful, crouch down, wave a stuffie at him, or turn and walk the other way so that he'll follow.
2. If he still doesn't come, don't repeat the

command but very, very gently tug on the leash. This should not be a jerk or a yank but merely a means to gently encourage him to start walking. (The beauty of a martingale collar, besides its pretty fabric, is that it won't hurt your Greyhound's throat if he tries to pull you—which sometimes he will—or if you must pull him.) Keep smiling, but stop gently tugging when he starts walking.

3. When he gets to you, reward him with a treat, praise, petting, and playing.

To ensure that he will identify the *come* as the happiest of commands, never use it for something he doesn't like, such as nail trimming, and never punish him when he comes to you. He may have done something naughty, but if you call and he comes, he's a good boy. Reward him.

Sit

Sit is a wonderful command because a sitting dog isn't doing anything annoying. Whether you're welcoming guests to the house, preparing your dog's meal, or getting ready to take him on a walk, the *sit* command (followed by *stay* or *wait*, which we'll come to later) prevents him from getting overexcited and jumpy.

Many retired racers like to sit. Others are uncomfortable sitting, and given that their rear-leg muscles are overdeveloped and their spines long, it's not surprising. My Earl could not be comfortable sitting,

The *stay* command tells your dog not to move until you release him.

so his *sit* was a little curtsy with his rear. Smart boy!

How to Teach *Sit*

1. With your Greyhound standing facing you, hold a treat right above his nose.
2. Say "Max, sit" and slowly move your hand back toward his tail. His head should follow the treat while his rear moves downward to a *sit*.
3. Whether he achieves a full *sit* or an approximation of one, he's earned the treat and praise. ("Good sit.")
4. Repeat the sequence, which is holding

One of the basic commands your Greyhound should learn is how to walk nicely on leash.

a treat above his nose, giving the command (just once), using the treat to guide him into a *sit*, and rewarding him when he sits or almost sits.

5. After a few repetitions, quit so that he won't get bored, but do another session later in the day.

When your dog has *sit* down pat, slowly increase the length of time he must sit to get his treat.

Stay or Wait

The *stay* command, or its alternative, *wait*, tells your dog not to move until you release him. This is a critically important command for your dog to know and should be used before he steps out the door for a walk, gets out of a car, or steps into an intersection. I use *wait* because to me *stay* implies a longer length of time, and I don't think that Greyhounds should be made to sit or stand still for very long. Remember to release your dog from *stay* or *wait* by saying "Okay."

How to Teach *Stay* or *Wait*

1. With your dog standing, sitting, or lying down, step in front of him, and holding a flattened palm to his face, sharply command "Stay" or "Wait."

TRAINING CHECKLIST

✓ To train successfully, be positive and consistent.

✓ Training should begin on Day 1 with housetraining.

✓ Socializing your dog to children and other dogs is a must.

✓ Learning basic commands will give your dog a foundation for a happy life.

2. If he moves, put him back in position but don't repeat the command. Have him remain still just a few seconds before you praise, treat, and release him.

3. Gradually increase the amount of time he stays still to earn his treat. (When the command precedes leaving the house or getting out of the car, he's too excited to need any reward except being released.)

Down

Teaching *down* instills even more self-control in a dog than *sit*. Don't confuse your dog by saying the word "down" when you mean "off." *Down* means that you want him to lie down right where he is. *Off* is for when you want him to get down from the sofa. Because your Greyhound has thin skin, little body fat, and no coat to speak of on his stomach, he may be uncomfortable lying on hard surfaces. As much as possible, save *down* for carpeted floor and grass. Also, to lie down is a submissive action that your dog may not feel comfortable doing in a public setting. Unless your Greyhound is a puppy, it may be easier to teach *down* at home than in obedience class.

How to Teach *Down*

1. Begin with your dog standing or sitting.

2. Holding a treat in front of his nose, slowly lower your hand to the floor and pull your hand forward while saying "Max, down." His head will follow the treat.

3. When his elbows touch the floor—which may take time—treat and praise him even though his fanny is still in the air.

4. Repeat several times. The goal, of course, is for your dog to have all four legs on the floor. Don't be discouraged; after a few training sessions, it will happen. Patience and treats are everything in dog training. Meanwhile, isn't he adorable with his fanny in the air?

Walk Nicely on Leash

When you bring your Greyhound home, the first thing you will do is walk him in the yard with his flat nylon leash attached to his martingale collar. If he was trained for racing, he already knows how to walk politely at your side. But being out in the world—not at the track—may make him forget his training and forge ahead, especially if he sees a squirrel. This and other annoying behaviors while walking are easy to correct.

How to Teach Walk Nicely on Leash

For your Greyhound's safety, always walk him with his leash looped around your wrist, wrapped around the palm of your hand two or three times, and held in place with your thumb and fingers. When he pulls, stop walking. He'll have to stop too. When he relaxes and the leash goes slack, praise him and resume walking. Eventually he'll learn that pulling on the leash means a pause in the walk. If he sees a squirrel and lunges, stop walking and with both hands hold the leash against your mid-section—your center of gravity. You're in control, and your dog isn't going anywhere. Conversely, if he's so engrossed in sniffing something that he won't budge, turn around and walk in the opposite direction. When he catches up, praise him and turn around to continue your walk.

You can also teach your Greyhound to heel on leash, which means to walk at your side in lockstep with you. When teaching *heel*, have tiny treats in your hand closest to him. This is called training with a food lure. It's the same method used to teach the *kennel*, *come*, *sit*, and *down*. Basically, you're making the training process a happy sport by rewarding your dog for obeying a command he doesn't understand yet.

1. If your dog walks on your left side, hold the leash in your right hand while taking up the slack in your left hand—which also holds the treat.
2. Bringing the yummy to his nose, say his name and the word "heel" in a bright, positive tone.
3. When he walks beside you, treat and praise him.
4. Continue walking just a short distance with him heeling.
5. To release him from the *heel*, say "Okay." Let him sniff around or just enjoy your petting him. Then begin again with him standing at your side and you saying his name and the word "heel," and treat him again when he does.

Heel is a good command, but don't make it a rigid rule. After all, walks are meant to be fun, grass exists to be sniffed, and life is short.

How to Find a Dog Trainer

To find the right trainer for your dog, get recommendations from your vet and other dog owners, especially Greyhound owners. You can also look for a trainer in your area by visiting the website of the Association of Pet Dog Trainers (APDT) at www.apdt.com.

A good trainer will love dogs and use positive methods to facilitate learning.

Before signing up for classes, meet the trainer if possible and ask whether you may visit a class to see how she works. Even if you can't meet in person, ask what her credentials are, whether she has worked with Greyhounds before, what training methods she uses, and how many dogs will be in the class. A small class size is a plus, gentleness coupled with an obvious affection for dogs is very important, and safe and secure surroundings are imperative. A good trainer should be willing to refund most of your money if after your dog's first class you feel that it isn't right for him.

Teaching your Greyhound good manners and basic commands will not only add to his happiness, self-confidence, and safety but will also prepare him for recreational pursuits the two of you can enjoy together. There's an exciting world of dog sports to be discovered, which we will talk about in Chapter 8.

Chapter 7

Solving Problems With Your Greyhound

ENCOURAGING A PUPPY

Puppies, by definition, really can't be naughty. They just have eager little teeth that must chew everything in sight and little puppy bladders that must be emptied often—including in the middle of the night. Never scold a puppy (or adult dog, for that matter) for needing the bathroom. Instead, reward and praise your pup every time he eliminates outside. Do this even if you're shivering in your pajamas and yawning.

One of the great pleasures of living with your Greyhound will be watching his personality unfold as he develops unique and endearing behaviors. But sometimes our dogs surprise us with behaviors that aren't endearing. Let's look at ways to get your Greyhound off to a good start in his new home and how to deal with problems that may occur.

So This Is My Forever Home!

Your new family member is entering a brand-new world. It's a confusing situation. He can tell that you like him and that this is a nice place. But it's a foreign place, and at first he'll need constant guidance from you. You are more than his new mom or dad. You are his teacher.

Teaching the Basics

To help your dog adjust to his new forever home, begin with the basics. Walk him on leash to his water bowl. Show him which door leads to the yard and what stairs are for if they are new to him. Some Greyhounds who have never experienced stairs will take to them readily. Others are nervous about them for just a few minutes, and some remain skeptical for a day or two. You may have to physically help your dog with the first steps, after which he will probably want to do it on his own—fast, to make it safely to the top where he can stand on all fours. Even if he has experience with stairs, your stairs are new and different. Having another dog present to demonstrate the ease and safety of stair climbing may make it easier. Having tasty tidbits in your pocket to reward his efforts at the top of the stairs and again at the bottom will also help. Just remember that coercion, or your acting nervous, will not get him to trust stairs—but praise from you in a soft and cheerful tone will.

Before your Greyhound moves in, you'll have to decide whether he's allowed on the furniture.

Handling New Noises

Noises from household appliances can be frightening to a dog without home experience. Instead of sympathizing or coddling—which reinforces fear—reward your Greyhound for getting past his fears. If your blow-dryer scares him, toss him treats while drying your hair, with each treat falling closer to you. When he stops being afraid and comes right up to you, substitute petting and praise for treats. Similarly, if you're out walking and a street sound scares him, don't take him back home. Continue walking and talking. Your cheerful voice tells him there's nothing to fear from the neighbor's lawnmower.

Learning About Furniture

Before your dog moves in, decide whether he's allowed on furniture. Think carefully because once a dog has napped on the sofa or slept in bed with you, he'll have a hard time understanding that he can't do it again.

Ask the Expert

GETTING HELP WITH A PROBLEM BEHAVIOR

—Lee Livingood, Certified Dog Behavior Consultant, International
Association of Animal Behavior Consultants (IAABC)

Look for a trainer or behavioral counselor who uses gentle, humane methods and avoids punishments. Interview the consultant. Ask about her training and background, what professional associations she belongs to, and how long she's been doing behavioral work. Does she do it full- or part-time? If part-time, is her other work in a related field? Ask how many dogs she works with each year and how many retired racers she's worked with. If she hasn't worked with Greyhounds, ask about other sighthounds and other adult rescues.

Ask specifically what training devices and techniques she uses. How does she feel about food in training? There are different approaches to training, and a good trainer will use a variety of techniques to get the approach that is right for you and your dog. But there are no situations where harsh physical or emotional punishments or corrections are appropriate.

Get references. Don't assume that the most expensive trainer is the best one, but don't shop for the cheapest one either. As one trainer so eloquently put it, "If you pay peanuts, you get to work with monkeys."

Many Greyhounds have no interest in getting on furniture. Others consider it their birthright. It may be best to withhold this privilege until your dog understands that his place in the pack is below all humans. How can he know that you're his leader if he's hogging the bed and has a paw on your pillow? If he starts to climb onto the sofa, say "Off" and gently guide him off. If you get up and he takes your place, say "Off," and with your hand on his collar, guide him off. Praise him the instant he has a foot on the floor.

Teaching *Give Up*

Along with basic commands, I teach my dogs *give up*, meaning "Let me have that." To teach *give up*, hold a treat in front of your dog's face, and with your free hand reach for what you want while saying "Give up." As the exchange is made, say "Good give up." Even after your dog has learned that what is his is really yours, continue to reward him each time he obeys "Give up."

Don't give a new dog anything you may have to take away later, such as a chew

If your dog is barking from loneliness, a second Greyhound might be just the solution.

treat that's becoming small enough to choke on. If you have a retired racer, he probably never had a toy of his own before and may growl when you reach for what he sees as his. If you must take a chewy from him, see whether he'll exchange it for a treat. If not, gently drape a towel over his head before taking the object. When you remove the towel, treat and praise him. This is a safe, easy way to protect your dog and yourself from unpleasant confrontation. He wants to be good in everything he does; he just doesn't know how yet.

Problem Behaviors

Curbing incorrect behavior is much the same as reinforcing correct behavior. Respond immediately so that your dog will know why he's being corrected. Use the same command each time the behavior occurs, and instantly reward him when he obeys.

Correcting a dog should not weaken his trust in you or undermine his self-confidence. Don't say his name in anger or do anything that could hurt him emotionally or physically. Without using his name, say "No!" for something utterly

THE LOST GREYHOUND

If suddenly your dog is loose and not in arm's reach, don't let him know that you're alarmed. If you're near your car, cheerfully call, "Car ride, Maxie!" while jiggling your keys and opening the door for him. If you have a squawker handy (See Chapter 3: Supplies for Your Greyhound), use it. Otherwise, get playful. Sit on the ground and call "Biscuit!" or "Treats!"—or call your dog's name while running away from him. If he bolts, or if he got loose without your knowing, start searching immediately. Take treats and his favorite squeaky toy and call to him with your happiest voice. If you don't find him in just a few minutes, phone everyone who will help search—including your adoption group and others in your area—and ask everyone to spread the word that he's missing. Ask your adoption group to form a search party—with Greyhounds included to help lure your dog out of hiding. Tell kids in the neighborhood that your dog is loose. Tell everyone his name so that they can call to him. Phone shelters and veterinarians throughout your area and nearby areas too, and if your dog is microchipped or has tattoos, give them this information. Ask friends to help you post flyers around your neighborhood, on store bulletins, in parks, and in schools (ask permission first) with a photo of your dog, his name, when and where he was lost, and phone numbers to call. (Be sure to remove the flyers after your dog is found.) Post to Internet discussion lists and bulletin boards, and ask readers to cross-post to other lists.

To be proactive, keep color photos of your dog in your car and store phone numbers in your cell phone to call if your dog gets loose.

unacceptable (jumping to get to the canary's cage), "Wrong!" for something inappropriate (jumping in excitement before a car ride), and "Off!" for having all or part of his body where it shouldn't be.

Greyhounds are sensitive and don't like being scolded. If you are firm and consistent in your corrections—never weakening your resolve because he looks so cute when he misbehaves—your dog will learn which behaviors are not acceptable. For every lapse that you witness, correct him. The moment he stops the unwanted behavior, calmly praise him. He'll catch on.

Barking

Barking is a behavior that, fortunately,

rarely becomes a problem for Greyhound owners.

How to Manage It

Most Greys don't bark or bark only to welcome whoever comes to the door—friend or thief, it doesn't matter. There are exceptions to the rule, though. One of my retired racers surprised me months after joining our family by barking up a storm whenever I was getting ready to take him for a walk or car ride. I didn't want this, so Bruce had to learn that if he barked when I was getting ready to take him out, I would turn my back on him and not move or speak until he was quiet. Now when I pick up his collar and leash and say "Collar," he knows that I want him to be quiet and hold still (or as still as he can, given his level of excitement) while I slip the collar over his head. When the collar is on, I praise him and off we go.

A dog isolated from his family may bark in loneliness, which you can and should prevent by putting his crate into the family area and his bed near yours. Being home alone causes some dogs to bark—that's separation anxiety. A happy solution for many families is to get a second Greyhound. But if that isn't on your agenda (at least not for a while), there are other means to calm him, which are discussed further in

this chapter. (See sidebar "Aggression and Separation Anxiety.")

Chewing

Puppies need to chew, and for most, the need turns into a lifelong love of chewing that helps them have healthier teeth. But you don't want your dog to use the coffee table to prevent tartar buildup!

How to Manage It

To keep your Greyhound from chewing on inappropriate items, give him chew toys that are size appropriate and don't contain parts he can break off and swallow. (Don't give him an old shoe to gnaw, or he may think that all shoes are for chewing.) Say "No!" when your dog reaches for something off-limits to him, then give him one of his squeaky toys. Bitter-tasting spray products to stop inappropriate chewing are available at pet supply stores and online.

Choose chew treats with care. Those made of compressed vegetable protein and fiber promote dental health, but pieces can lodge in the gastrointestinal tract, creating a potentially fatal danger. Rawhides become soft and gooey when chewed and when swallowed can cause an obstruction in the throat or esophagus. The solution? Research the relative safety of chew treats before buying them, and stay near your

AGGRESSION AND SEPARATION ANXIETY

Greyhounds rarely show aggression toward humans. When it happens, it's either fear related from a past trauma or lack of socialization; health related, possibly from pain or hypothyroidism; or a dominance issue, with the dog thinking that he's alpha (first in order of importance) in the family. Greyhounds sometimes growl a little in play. This isn't aggression. Nor is the famous Greyhound grin, which shows a lot of teeth. Aggression presents itself as serious growling, guarding possessions, snapping, or biting. It's extremely unlikely that an aggressive Greyhound would be made available for adoption.

Separation anxiety can occur with any dog who craves human companionship, especially when there's not another dog in the family. Greyhounds do love their humans, but usually their separation anxiety is mild and resolves itself in time. To minimize the chance of separation anxiety, never kennel your dog without giving him a treat, and consider giving him his meals in the crate. Also, crate him at other times when you're not leaving the house. Vary the amount of time your dog is crated and you're not home so that he won't know whether you're leaving for a minute or an hour. Leave a radio on, tuned to easy-listening music. A durable rubber toy stuffed with peanut butter will keep the dog occupied until he's ready for a snooze.

If your Greyhound is aggressive or has severe separation anxiety, seek help from a certified dog behavior consultant, credentialed canine behaviorist, or trainer who uses humane methods to effect change.

Greyhound when he has an ingestible chewy between his paws. Toys made of durable rubber are safe for most dogs, and when filled with peanut butter and small treats can help alleviate separation anxiety.

Counter Surfing
Long in leg, body, and neck, Greyhounds probably invented counter surfing. Tall males are the worst, but a nimble female can grab a sandwich you'd have sworn was beyond her reach and get it to her crate before you can yell "Stop, thief!" Obviously, you won't leave food near the front of a counter or on a table and walk out of the room (even to answer the doorbell), leaving your dog alone to guard the yummies.

If your Greyhound is digging in your garden, give him an alternative place to dig.

I prepare people meals but only after they've learned not to beg or steal. And to get their treat, they must obey at least one command. Sometimes I have them do the "sit, down, kennel up" dance.

Digging

Digging is another problem behavior that isn't usually a problem for Greyhound owners.

How to Manage It

Inappropriate digging in the yard won't be an issue unless you leave your dog outside unsupervised, which isn't wise to do with a Greyhound. Dogs dig holes to uncover what smells so interesting, to bury a possession, to have a cool place to rest on a hot day, or to escape because they're bored and lonely. You can designate a special spot for your dog to dig, or with verbal correction ("Wrong") and positive reinforcement (the treats in your pocket), you can teach him not to dig. Fill in the hole he's started, cover it with a flowerpot or chair, and play with him or take him inside.

House Soiling

A completely housetrained dog will not eliminate indoors without cause. If your Greyhound has a sudden bout of diarrhea and you aren't there to get him outside fast enough, he has no choice in the matter.

How to Manage It

Start teaching *off* the first time your Greyhound lifts his nose to sniff the table or counter. As you firmly command "Off!" gently push his face away. Then reward him with a cheerful "Good off"—but don't treat him. If your dog isn't fed anything in the kitchen except *his* meal from *his* bowl, he won't have expectations that lead to problem behaviors. I admit to sometimes giving my dogs tidbits while

SOLVING PROBLEM BEHAVIORS CHECKLIST

✓ Solve problems before they occur by teaching basic good behavior.

✓ Discourage normal behavior that can be hurtful to humans, such as jumping and nitting.

✓ Curb incorrect behavior swiftly, calmly, and with positive reinforcement.

✓ When things get out of hand, consult a behaviorist.

How to Manage It

If house soiling isn't a one-time occurrence, take your dog to the vet, as he may have intestinal parasites or another health issue. If his soiling indoors isn't health related, he may need more and longer bathroom breaks than he's getting. Most dogs don't walk out the door and immediately relieve themselves. They require stimulation and will trot back and forth across the yard—stopping to sniff smells from the past—before eliminating. Lapses in housetraining can also be caused by turmoil in the home or from separation anxiety. They also can occur in old age from canine cognitive dysfunction syndrome (CDS) (see Chapter 9), when the dog simply forgets his housetraining.

Some male dogs mark their new territory without distinguishing between its exterior and interior. Indoor marking can usually be curtailed by watching the dog closely the first few days. If he starts to lift a leg, correct him with a firm "No!" and take him outside. If the problem persists, a doggy bellyband, available online and in some pet supply stores, will help with persistent marking. The cloth band, which isn't meant to be worn constantly, feels comfortable to the dog until it gets wet. When he learns that marking indoors makes him uncomfortable, he won't want to do it. (Be sure to rule out ill health as a cause of indoor urination before buying a bellyband for your boy.)

After any house soiling, clean the area and use a natural deodorizer on the spot so that your dog won't be drawn to it again.

Jumping Up

Greyhounds love greeting people by jumping up on them. It's a sweet welcome unless your blouse gets raked by his nails or Grandma gets knocked off her feet. If your dog's love of jumping up is greater than his wish to obey your "Wrong!" or "Off!," there are other ways to correct him.

How to Manage It

One way to manage jumping up is to fold

your arms over your chest when your dog starts to jump and silently turn away from him. Remain stone-like until he's still, then softly praise and pet him. If he jumps again, give him the cold shoulder again. He'll soon learn that jumping won't gain him the attention he wants.

Another method is to take hold of your dog's front feet when he jumps up and slowly walk forward. He won't like walking backward on two feet and will be glad when you let go. Again, pet and quietly praise him when he's on all fours.

Whichever method you choose, use it consistently and have family members do the same. Tell children not to push the dog away if he jumps up, as he'll think that they're playing. Until he's well trained, have him on leash when guests arrive.

Marking

Some male dogs mark their new territory without distinguishing between its exterior and interior. This is scent marking, not peeing.

How to Manage It

Marking can usually be curtailed by watching the dog closely the first few days. If he starts to lift a leg, correct him with a firm "No!" and take him outside. If the problem becomes continuous, a doggy bellyband, available online and in some pet supply stores, will help with persistent marking. The cloth band, which isn't meant to be worn constantly, feels comfortable to the dog until it gets wet. When he learns that marking indoors makes him uncomfortable, he won't want to do it. (Be sure to rule out ill health as a cause of indoor urination before buying a bellyband for your boy.)

After any house soiling, clean the area and use a natural deodorizer on the spot so that your dog won't be drawn to it again.

Nitting, not Nipping

Greyhounds aren't likely to nip or mouth you in play, as many breeds will, but some

Discourage nitting if your Greyhound is inclined to do so, and warn children never to put their hands near a dog's mouth.

Some thunderphobic dogs feel a buildup of static charge during a storm, which is physically and mentally discomforting.

Greys will "nit" at your fingers with their front teeth when happy and excited. This is like having your finger caught between chattering teeth. The dog only wants to share his joy, but it can be painful.

How to Manage It

Discourage the habit by saying "Wrong" and turning away from your dog. And warn children not to put their hands near any dog's mouth. They should be taught this whether the dog nits or not.

Thunderphobia

Fear of thunder isn't a bad-behavior-related problem, but it is a problem. Some dogs are just scared by the noise, in which case desensitization techniques may help. But others feel a buildup of static charge, which is physically and mentally discomforting. Such dogs may seek comfort in a bathroom or laundry area when they sense a storm coming, as the metal pipes in these areas act as electrical grounding devices. If your dog is thunderphobic, help him find comfort during a storm without reinforcing his fear by coddling. And be sure that the dog doesn't wedge himself into a tight spot from which he'll have trouble getting out.

How to Manage It

There are several ways to help a thunderphobic dog, so you may have to experiment or combine treatments. The Storm Defender Cape—with a metallic lining that discharges a dog's fur and shields him from static charge buildup—works for many dogs. Some dogs won't keep the cape on, though. The Anxiety Wrap, essentially a compression garment, can't be shaken off but is a bit tricky to get the dog into at first. Melatonin, a mildly sedating supplement found in health stores, may also help. Ask your vet before giving melatonin, and don't give it to a dog who has severe allergies or an autoimmune disease. Comfort Zone with D.A.P.—a dog-appeasing pheromone used to prevent fear and separation anxiety—works wonders for my thunderphobic Minnie. (A company representative said to purchase the spray, not the plug in, and to spray Minnie's bedding at least ten minutes before she used it.) Also soothing is easy-listening music from a radio placed near the dog.

One method of desensitization is to snuggle up with your dog for an hour or so, several days in a row, while sounds of recorded storms fill the house. Herbal remedies such as PetCalm or Rescue Remedy, which are commonly used for dogs who have separation anxiety, might help. Like any other product recommended by veterinarians or Greyhound breeders or trainers, use these according to directions. Desensitization alone won't work for a dog who suffers static buildup in his fur but may work in combination with having his coat rubbed with an unscented fabric-softener dryer sheet.

How to Find a Behaviorist

If your dog has a behavior problem that isn't caused by a medical condition and isn't being resolved by obedience training, your next course of action is to hire a professional canine behaviorist. Get recommendations from your vet, adoption group, or humane society. Don't respond to a print or online ad, as anyone can claim to be a behaviorist or trainer. The American College of Veterinary Behaviorists (ACVB) is a resource for finding board-certified veterinary behaviorists. But a superb dog trainer needn't be a vet—just someone who's qualified and experienced and loves dogs.

Problem behaviors can occur with any dog. They're not the dog's fault, and they're not the owner's fault if the owner is a conscientious person like yourself. (If you weren't, you wouldn't be reading a breed book.) Just take it one step at a time, get outside help if necessary, and remember that your dog loves you.

Chapter
8

Activities With
Your Greyhound

Greyhounds love being out and about, and there's a wealth of activities—social, competitive, contributing to society, and just plain fun—that you and your dog can enjoy together. In this chapter we'll look at just a few of the many activities in which your Grey can participate, as well as safety and travel tips.

Competitive Sports and Events

Although your Greyhound was bred and is built for speed and can make split-second turns, he is also by design a couch potato. Before being engaged in any athletic exercise, he should have a physical checkup, then be eased into the sport slowly. Keep in mind that he's not built to run or jump on hard surfaces, that he mustn't be overheated or kept in direct sun very long, and that injuries can permanently alter a dog's quality of life. Warm-ups are required before each performance, and exercise should never occur within two hours of the dog having eaten. And it goes without saying that even in competition your Greyhound must not be off leash in an unsecured area.

Agility

Agility, a sport that began in England in 1978, is one of the fastest-growing dog sports in the United States. The first agility trial held by the American Kennel Club (AKC) was in 1994.

In agility trials, dogs compete by running off leash through a series of obstacles to see who can complete the course the fastest. The course must be finished in a specified time without knocking over a jump pole or missing an obstacle. Agility training builds confidence and is a great way for you and your dog to exercise together. (Yes, you'll be running too, but you won't have to negotiate the ramps and tunnels.)

Conformation (Dog Shows)

A conformation show is an event in which dogs are evaluated against their breed standard. Conformation (dog showing) is open to dogs with reproductive organs intact who are registered with breed parent clubs such as the AKC and, in England, the Kennel Club (KC). (The dog may participate only in shows sponsored by his club.) Comparatively few Greyhounds are registered with these clubs, and of those registered, not all are of show caliber. (This doesn't mean that your AKC-registered Grey who holds one ear in a whimsical position isn't the most gorgeous dog who ever lived. He is.)

Conformation is a sport the whole family can enjoy, but it's not for everyone. Attend a few shows in your area and see whether this is your cup of tea. If so, get opinions on whether your dog is of show caliber before entering any, as dog showing can be very

PUPPY ACTIVITIES

The main activities of Greyhound puppies are eating, chewing things not meant to be eaten, and running. Greyhounds are extremely fast, have energy to spare, and need lots of exercise. During this time, the most important activity to concentrate on is leash training using a martingale collar. Play fetch too, but choose only soft toys for a puppy, as his mouth and teeth are not as strong as an adult dog's.

expensive. It must be mentioned that this is one of the few sports in which amateurs and professionals compete against one another. Your best resource is the AKC's New Exhibitor Mentoring Program, which matches experienced dog fanciers and breeders with recent registrants of AKC dogs or those thinking of getting an AKC dog. Who knows whether your Greyhound—if spirited, quick to learn, and with the proper gait (quality of movement)—will climb the ladder, winning one class and competition after another, to become the first Greyhound to win Best in Show in America.

Canine Freestyle

Canine freestyle is a sport in which handler and dog move in a choreographed set of moves set to music. You create a dance routine, teach it to your Greyhound, and together you perform it to music. This sport provides an opportunity for you to have a willing dance partner who doesn't step on your toes or want to dance with anyone else. You may enter competitions or dance for your own pleasure. Either way, freestyle will deepen your bond with your Grey, reinforce your training skills, and give you great joy. *"Tango, Maxie?"*

Lure Coursing

When Cleopatra's Greyhounds competed as open field coursers, they chased after a hare. In today's coursing competitions, the lure is without feelings, and the sport is as thrilling to watch as it is humane. Lure coursing is for dogs in excellent condition—including being at optimal weight, which for a retired racer is within 5 pounds (2.5 kg) of racing weight—and without past injuries. But if your Greyhound's daily exercise consists of short walks interrupted by lots of tree sniffing, he's not ready for coursing even if you can see a few ribs and the tips of his hip bones. A vet exam to determine his condition is a wise choice before he takes the leap into this rigorous sport.

Lure coursing tests a dog's ability to hunt by sight or coursing instinct.

The several types of lure coursing, which you can research on the Internet, are purely for fun, with no betting or cash prizes allowed. In AKC lure coursing, judges score the dogs on agility, endurance, enthusiasm, speed, and ability to follow the lure. Up to three dogs run together on two courses varying from 600 to 1,000 yards (548.5 to 914.5 m), and the combined score of both courses determines the winner. Additional runs may be necessary in the case of ties and to decide Best of Breed and Best in Field. Dogs wear a colored coursing blanket and a quick-release collar. Racing muzzles are optional. A hound earns his Junior Courser title when certified to compete,

then goes on to earn the Senior Courser, Master Courser, and Field Champion titles. (More information is available at www. akc.org/events/lure_coursing.)

American Sighthound Field Association (ASFA) lure coursing is very similar to AKC coursing and is also run with up to three dogs on a field, with racing muzzles optional. In addition to Best of Breed and Best in Field, dogs compete for the Field Champion and Lure Courser of Merit titles. (For more information, go to www.asfa.org.)

The Large Gazehound Racing Association (LGRA) has the hounds race 200 yards (183 m) on a straight, flat track after a furry lure with a squawker inside. They are graded according to previous racing experience or using the LGRA "WAVE," a weighted average of the dog's last three race meets. A maximum of four hounds wearing properly fitted muzzles compete in three programs. Winners earn points towards the Gazehound Racing Champion title, requiring 12 points. After this title is achieved, the hound earns points toward the Superior Gazehound Racing Champion title (30 points). (For more information, go to www.lgra.org.)

The National Oval Track Racing Association (NOTRA) has Greyhounds race muzzled on an oval or horseshoe-shaped track that varies between 220 and 440 meters. This is a speed-based event, with the fastest dog over three courses declared the winner. Up to four Greys compete at a time for the Junior Oval Racer title, the Senior Oval Racer, the Oval Racing Champion, and the Supreme Oval Racing Champion. (For more information, go to www.notra.org.)

Rally

Rally is a newer sport that the AKC rightly claims is taking the nation by storm. Defined as a stepping stone from the AKC Canine Good Citizen test to obedience or agility competition, rally allows dogs and their handlers to proceed at their own pace through a course of 10 to 20 designated stations, with a sign at each station indicating what maneuver the dog-handler team is supposed to do. While handlers may not touch their dog or make physical corrections, they are encouraged to communicate with the dog by talking, praising, encouraging, clapping hands, and patting their legs. Because most of us do all of the above at home with our Greyhounds, and our dogs thrive on praise and encouragement, rally is definitely a sport to consider. The purpose of rally is to produce dogs that have been trained to behave at home, in public, and in the presence of other dogs in a manner that will reflect positively on the sport.

To be eligible to compete in AKC rally trials, your dog must be six months or older and registered with the AKC or listed with the AKC Purebred Alternative Listing/Indefinite Listing Privilege (PAL/ILP) program.

Canine Good Citizen® Program

The Canine Good Citizen (CGC) program, with no age limits and open to both purebred and mixed breeds, was developed by the AKC to promote responsible pet ownership. After you've trained your dog to obey basic commands and behave politely with other dogs and people, he may take the CGC test. Before a dog takes the Canine Good Citizen test, his owner signs the Responsible Dog Owners Pledge. With this you agree to take care of your dog's health, safety, exercise, training, and quality of life. Also, you agree to show

GREYHOUNDS IN SPORTS

—Laurel Drew, breeder, trainer, and archivist for the
Greyhound Club of America (GCA)

Greyhounds enjoy a variety of sports but do better at some than others. Lure coursing and agility are two sports in which Greyhounds excel, as the dogs can use their speed and agility to the fullest. Although Greyhounds can succeed in obedience, they do not often score in the top ranks. Rally tests are more to a Greyhound's liking than obedience because they provide a series of stations at which the dog must perform a specific exercise, but you are on your own and can take as long as you need to perform the maneuver. Rally also requires more agility in the turns than does obedience. If you are considering any of these sports, look for a Greyhound who is agile, lively, and in some cases actually mischievous. I prefer a female because males, in general, are more laid-back. Although they are steady, they do not always have the flash and fire the females have to make good times and to excite the judges.

responsibility by such actions as cleaning up after him in public places and never letting him infringe on the rights of others. When you have signed it, you and your dog are ready to take the CGC test, which includes the following steps:

Test 1: *Accepting a friendly stranger* demonstrates that the dog will allow a friendly stranger to approach him and speak to the handler in a natural, everyday situation.

Test 2: *Sitting politely for petting* demonstrates that the dog will allow a friendly stranger to touch him while he is out with his handler.

Test 3: *Appearance and grooming* demonstrates that the dog will welcome being groomed and examined by someone other than the owner.

Test 4: *Out for a walk (walking on a loose lead)* demonstrates that the handler is in control of the dog.

Test 5: *Walking through a crowd* demonstrates that the dog can move about politely in pedestrian traffic and is under control in public places.

Test 6: *Sit and down on command and staying in place* demonstrates that the dog has training, will respond to the handler's commands to sit and down, and will remain in the place commanded by the handler.

Test 7: *Coming when called* demonstrates that the dog will come when called by the handler, who walks 10 feet (3 m) from the dog, turns to face him, and then calls the dog to come.

Test 8: *Reaction to another dog* demonstrates that the dog can behave politely around other dogs.

Test 9: *Reaction to distraction* demonstrates that the dog is confident when faced with common distracting situations, such as having a jogger run in front of him.

Test 10: *Supervised separation* demonstrates a dog's willingness to be left with a trusted person and maintain training and good manners.

(You can see the ten steps in full on the AKC's website, www.akc.org.)

Throughout the testing, dogs may not be shown or given food, treats, or toys. While these rewards are useful during the training process, they are a no-no on the big day. And what a big day it is! I know from experience that having your dog awarded the CGC title makes *you* feel like a good citizen too.

Greyhound Meet and Greets

Taking your dog to Greyhound meet and greets will help satisfy his need for socialization while allowing him to be

Greyhound meet and greets allow the dogs to enjoy each other's company.

THE INDEFINITE LISTING PRIVILEGE (ILP)

If your Greyhound isn't a show dog, he can still participate in other American Kennel Club (AKC) events. As long as he is purebred (all retired racers are), age six months or older, and spayed or neutered, you may apply for the AKC's Indefinite Listing Privilege (ILP). With the ILP, your Grey can compete in agility, obedience, and rally trials, as well as junior showmanship and tracking tests. Complete information is available at www.akc.org.

an ambassador for his breed. Held by adoption groups throughout the year at venues as diverse as the public park and the mall pet shop, meet and greets serve three purposes. The dogs enjoy the company of their own kind and being petted by admiring people, Greyhound owners get to see old friends and make new ones, and passersby who stop to meet our dogs and learn about them often are inspired to add a Greyhound to their own family.

Your adoption group may host several meet and greets each month and may have a walking club as well. Almost certainly it has an annual reunion picnic, open to the public, with Greyhounds numbering in the fifties or hundreds. You may discover that you're within easy driving range of annual picnics held by several groups. If your dog is an AKC Greyhound, not a retired racer, by all means take him to events held by Greyhound adoption groups. The people there will probably recognize your dog as AKC bred and will be delighted to meet

him. After all, most of us don't get to see AKC Greyhounds except on television.

And if you enjoy traveling, you can attend Greyhound reunions that draw attendees from across the United States. The largest, "Greyhounds Reach the Beach," in Dewey Beach, Delaware, is attended each fall by thousands of retired racers and their owners.

Therapy Work

If you enjoy volunteering and your dog likes meeting people, you can team up to bring comfort and cheer to people in nursing homes and other institutions where care is provided. Everything about the Greyhound, from his quiet demeanor to his oh-so-soft coat, makes this breed highly suitable as a therapy dog.

Therapy Dogs International, Inc. (TDI) has dogs working throughout the United States and Canada. To be certified, a dog must be at least a year old, have earned the Canine Good Citizen title, have a health record form signed by a veterinarian, and be tested and evaluated for behavior

Everything about the Greyhound, including his quiet demeanor, makes him highly suitable as a therapy dog.

around people who use service equipment, such as a wheelchair or crutches. TDI even has a program in which dogs help children learn to read. You can read all about it at www.tdi-dog.org.

The Delta Society (www.deltasociety. org) is a human-services organization dedicated to improving people's health and well-being through positive interactions with animals. Several programs are offered, including Delta Society's Pet Partners Program, which trains and screens volunteers and their pets for visiting animal programs in hospitals, nursing homes, rehabilitation centers, schools, and other facilities.

Tricks and Treats

Teaching your dog to play games and do tricks will provide exercise and mental stimulation even when inclement weather keeps you indoors. Start with playing catch. Greyhounds—being sighthounds and food motivated—are great at this. Who needs a tennis ball and being outdoors when a handful of kibble and a little space will do?

Treats on Toes

A dog who knows *down* and *wait* (see Chapter 6) can learn the "treats on toes"

No matter what sport you and your Greyhound choose, it should be a fun experience for both of you.

trick. With your Grey in the *down* position, use your left hand to place a tiny treat on the indentation between his second and third toes. While giving the *wait* signal with your right hand, say "Wait." Lift your hand but remain with your back bent in case you need to stop your dog from grabbing the treat. He should only have to wait a couple of seconds before you say "Okay" to release him. Gradually increase the length of time he has to wait to get his reward, but be reasonable. Later you can teach him to play the game with treats balanced on both front feet. My Sequel wowed the judges with this trick and won the first place trophy at a Greyhound Pets of America picnic.

Dance of the Treat Ball

All you need to play this game is a Greyhound, a stuffable treat ball (available at pet supply stores), and a handful of small kibble or toasted oat cereal. Fill the ball with the treats and put it on the floor. Let the dance begin!

Travel and Vacationing

Anytime you travel with your dog, plan ahead so that the trip will be as stress-free and safe as possible. A vet visit before you go, to make sure that your dog is in good health, is also wise.

Packing for the Greyt Adventure

Packing for your dog is actually more

Check It Out

ACTIVITY PARTICIPATION CHECKLIST

✓ Choose activities suited to your Greyhound's personality and temperament.

✓ Be sure that you and your dog are in good condition before engaging in strenuous activity.

✓ If an activity isn't fun for your dog, it's not the right one for him.

✓ When traveling with your Greyhound, have vital information and phone numbers with you. Be prepared for the possibility of sickness, injury, or your dog's getting loose. If at all possible, avoid airplane travel.

important than packing for yourself because you'll do fine without food, bowls, favorite toys, and a bed from home. Make a list of everyday items your Grey will need on the trip—from poop bags to any medication he takes—and also of what may be needed: his basic first-aid kit (see Chapter 9) or first-aid kit for hiking and camping (see Chapter 3), medical records (including proof of vaccinations), and printouts of Greyhound anesthesia guidelines and blood work. You'll also want contact information for veterinarians and emergency clinics near where you'll be staying. Take an ample supply of food, treats, and bottled water (or water from home, as the water where you're going may not agree with him). Ginger snaps will help prevent carsickness. And have current pictures of your dog and identifying information (ear tattoos and microchip number and

the registry phone number) in case he gets lost.

Finding Pet-Friendly Lodging

Wherever you go, arrange for pet-friendly lodgings and confirm your reservation before setting out. Also ask about extra pet fees or deposits, where your dog can be walked, and whether he's allowed in the lobby. Some lodgings allow dogs in smoking rooms only, so if this would be a problem for you, be sure to ask. You can find pet-friendly accommodations by contacting the chamber of commerce or visitor's information center in the area you'll be visiting or by checking online directories. Be sure to obey the rules of places you visit with your pup, and don't leave him alone in the room. A Greyhound who never has separation anxiety at home can experience it away from home.

When traveling with your dog, plan ahead to make the trip a pleasant one.

Methods of Transportation

Whether you're traveling by car or plane, the most important thing is to keep your Greyhound safe for the duration of the journey.

By Car

The ideal way for your Greyhound to travel by car is for him to be in a crate bungee corded to the back seat or restrained in the back by a harness or doggy seat belt. Any of these will keep him from flying forward during a sudden stop or in an accident. Car barriers made of nylon mesh or metal to keep dogs in the back seat are of limited value, as striking metal will seriously injure a dog, and mesh isn't likely to hold up in an accident. So go with the crate, harness, or seat belt. And never let your dog ride in the front seat—a deployed air bag can kill him. Something else you never want to do is leave your dog alone in a car—even for just a few minutes, even on a cool day—with the doors locked and a window cracked. The risks aren't worth the convenience.

By Plane

If your vacation involves air travel, it would be best not to include your Greyhound. Large dogs can be shipped by air, but even though they're in a pressurized, climate-controlled compartment of the plane, it's highly stressful and never without risk. There can be delays, canceled flights, a dog kept crated for too long or left on the tarmac in hot weather—or becoming ill in flight with no one to know. Show Greyhounds are almost always driven to shows in vans or motor homes, and some handlers would forgo a show rather than have the dog travel by plane.

If you must ship your Grey by plane, you'll need an airline-approved crate with absorbent padding. A pail filled with frozen water (which won't spill during loading) attached to the inside of the crate will keep him hydrated during the flight. Do not sedate your dog before flying unless absolutely necessary, as evidence shows that sedation increases the risk of injury and death. Really, your Greyhound would be better off being boarded while you take your vacation. You can bring him presents and give him extra attention when you return.

Traveling With Kids

Being behind the wheel of a car with children and a large dog as passengers is a big responsibility, but with planning the trip can be safe and fun for all. When getting into the car and whenever you come to a stop, your Greyhound is likely to be excited. Excitement is stressful, so it's important that children behave calmly and not increase his stress level. Encourage them to speak softly to him, and petting should be very gentle. In between "starts" and "stops," the road slipping away under your Grey's tummy will probably lull him into sleep. Remind the kids not to disturb his rest, not to share their treats with him, not to unsnap his seat belt or open his crate, and to never open the car door until you give the okay. It's chilling even to imagine a Greyhound being lost far from home.

Traveling With the Senior Greyhound

A Greyhound in his senior years can still enjoy traveling with his family, but he may need more frequent bathroom breaks, some help getting in and out of the car, and extra cushioning to absorb the road bumps. He may also tire more easily and be more sensitive to cold and heat than when he was young. Be attentive to all of his needs, including seeing that he gets plenty of fresh water. If he's on medication or a special diet, calculate how much he'll need for the trip—and to be safe, take along more than he needs.

With so many opportunities for enriching our dogs' lives and our own through activities we can do together, there need never be a dull day. Even better, by engaging in just one activity that includes other people and dogs, new friendships will result that may last a lifetime. Greyhounds love making friends!

Chapter
9

Health of
Your Greyhound

After his family, a dog's best friend is his veterinarian. Your Greyhound will live a happier life if you provide him with quality medical care. This includes an annual physical examination and taking him to the vet when he shows signs of illness or injury. Just one of the advantages of routine veterinary care is that in an emergency situation, your Greyhound will have a doctor who knows him well and whom he already trusts.

Finding the Right Vet—or Vets

Greyhounds are even more unique on the inside than the outside. For your vet to correctly diagnose and treat your dog, she must have knowledge of his anatomical differences. Here are just a few. A Greyhound's heart is larger than the heart of other dogs of the same size, and his heart rate is slower. He has a lower percentage of body fat, making him much more sensitive to anesthesia. His blood values are different. For example, creatinine (a breakdown product of creatine, which is found in blood and muscle and excreted in urine) is higher in Greyhounds than in other dogs because of Greyhounds' large and lean muscle mass. A vet who doesn't know this may think that your dog is going into kidney failure when he's not. The vet must also know that low-grade heart murmurs are

common in Greyhounds and seldom signal a problem. The list of differences between Greyhounds and other breeds is long, and your dog requires medical care from someone who understands the differences.

Greyhound adoption groups and Greyhound breeders have veterinarians they trust. So if you acquired your dog from a local adoption group or breeder, you know someone who is well acquainted with a Greyhound-savvy vet. If you got your Greyhound at an animal shelter, you can still solicit a vet recommendation from an adoption group in your area. You may also take your Greyhound to two vets: one at arm's reach for routine visits and problems that must be addressed quickly and a Greyhound specialist who isn't nearby. Ask friends and neighbors to recommend a vet in your community. A vet who never met a Greyhound before can give your dog excellent care if she is eager to learn about Greyhounds and will confer with a vet who has Greyhound patients.

The First Vet Visit

After getting your Greyhound, take him to your veterinarian so that they can become acquainted and so that your dog's new doctor can evaluate his health. If your dog is a retired racer, he recently underwent a physical exam that most likely included testing for heartworm, intestinal parasites, and two tick-borne diseases: Lyme

The right vet for your dog should understand how Greyhounds differ anatomically from other breeds.

disease and ehrlichiosis. While he was under anesthesia for neutering, his teeth were examined and cleaned. Make a copy of the health records provided by your adoption group and give it to your veterinarian.

If you get a Greyhound puppy, take him to a vet for a health evaluation as soon as possible, as not all problems become obvious through mere observation. Besides examining your puppy, the vet will administer any vaccinations that are due. This would be a good time to discuss a vaccination schedule for your dog.

The Annual Vet Visit

All dogs need to see their doctor for an annual checkup. Your veterinary clinic will probably send you a postcard to remind you when it's time to schedule your Greyhound's annual visit. (Of course, anytime that you suspect something is wrong is time to see the vet. Don't allow a small problem to become serious.)

At the annual visit, your dog will be examined from head to tail. The vet will check his eyes, ears, nose, mouth (including teeth), skin, and coat. The vet will check his heart and lungs using a stethoscope, palpate his abdomen and groin area, and feel along the length of his spine. She will also feel his feet and nails.

Hospitalization

Dogs sometimes need hospitalization, and veterinarians are often reluctant to send hospitalized dogs home before they've eaten. But Greyhounds are very sensitive and should not remain hospitalized for

this reason alone. Tell your vet that you want to take your boy home where you can spoil him with your great cooking and that you'll bring him in for daily rechecks if needed.

Pet Insurance

You may wish to purchase health insurance for your Greyhound because dogs, like people, get sick and need routine checkups. Ask your vet and other dog owners to recommend insurance companies, then compare rates and find out what's covered and what isn't in the policies offered. If your dog has a

IS MY DOG SICK?

If your dog is crying from pain but you can't find signs of an injury, something is wrong and he needs veterinary care. Although some illnesses are subtle, you can gauge your Greyhound's health, whatever his age, by his appetite and attitude. If he looks sick and refuses to eat—even oatmeal cooked with butter and brown sugar and offered from your fingertips—he's sick. Get him to the vet. If it's after hours, go to the emergency clinic. Puppies and seniors are especially vulnerable to illness.

To protect your dog from household products that can poison him, go through your house and garage to make sure that there are no toxic substances that he can get into. Be especially careful about antifreeze, cleaning and deodorizing products, and medications. Make certain, too, that your yard doesn't harbor plants that are toxic to dogs. There are many; some can make your dog slightly ill if eaten, while others can be fatal. The websites of the Humane Society of the United States (HSUS) and the American Society for the Prevention of Cruelty to Animals (ASPCA) are but two of the many online resources for identifying plants that are dangerous to dogs.

pre-existing condition, you don't want a policy that excludes it. Most companies offer basic and upgraded plans. If you have more than one pet, ask the insurer whether a multiple-pet discount is offered. Know what you're buying so that there will be less chance of your being disappointed.

Spaying and Neutering

Racing Greyhounds are spayed or neutered after retirement and before being adopted, so if you adopt a retired racer the job is already done. Be glad, because "altered" dogs are much less likely to get certain cancers (prostate in males; ovarian and breast in females). Spaying and neutering also prevents "oops litters" and reduces aggressive tendencies. However, don't be fooled into thinking that altering a Greyhound makes his getting loose less dangerous to him, as his sight and speed will not be affected. If you purchase a puppy but don't intend to show or breed him, he should be neutered between six months to a year in age. For males, the testicles are removed (but your boy is still a guy), and females have their ovaries and uterus removed.

Vaccinations

The subject of vaccinating our dogs is controversial and likely to remain so, but vaccines are necessary to protect our best friends from certain diseases.

Racing Greyhounds are spayed or neutered after retirement and before being adopted.

Vaccinations usually begin at six weeks of age and continue to be given throughout the dog's life or until he's very old. The rabies vaccine is mandatory, as rabies—a viral infection that attacks the nervous system and can be spread to any mammal, including humans—can result in death. However, the rabies vaccine shouldn't be given at the same time as other vaccinations. You may want to schedule all vaccines a couple of weeks apart to reduce the risk of soreness or a possible reaction. Nevertheless, a single combination vaccine can ward off many diseases that your Greyhound should be protected against. They are:

PUPPY PROTECTION

If your Greyhound is a puppy, his best protection against health problems is a proper diet, being kept safe from harm, and regular care from his veterinarian.

- **Bordetella**, also called "kennel cough," which causes a nagging, raspy cough but generally isn't fatal. Boarding facilities only accept dogs protected against bordetella.
- **Canine coronavirus**, a viral infection that affects the intestinal tract.
- **Distemper**, a disease that can cause diarrhea, vomiting, pneumonia, and neurological problems. Distemper can be fatal.
- **Hepatitis**, a viral disease that affects the kidneys, liver, lungs, and spleen.
- **Leptospirosis**, another disease that affects the kidneys and liver; it can spread to humans.
- **Parainfluenza,** an infection of the upper respiratory system, is highly contagious among dogs.

There is a vaccine for Lyme disease, but it provides only short-term immunity, so annual revaccination is recommended. Some veterinarians believe that the vaccine may predispose the dog to Lyme nephritis, a rare but severe complication of Lyme disease. Because of this, the vaccine is controversial even in areas where ticks are common. (A new vaccine released recently may be a significant improvement. However, at the time of this writing it is too soon for a full evaluation.)

Many vets and a majority of veterinary schools now recommend repeating vaccinations every three years rather than annually or every two years. Don't vaccinate a dog who is sick, injured, pregnant, or nursing. Even the rabies vaccine may be waived for a very ill or infirm dog whose vet certifies that the dog never goes out and as such has zero risk of getting rabies. The American Animal Hospital Association (AAHA), an international association of more than 36,000 veterinarians, recommends that you ask your vet about the efficacy and duration of recommended vaccines. You will also need to check with your city or town.

Breed-Specific Illnesses

Veterinarians generally concur that overall the Greyhound is a healthy breed. But like all other breeds, the Greyhound is vulnerable to some hereditary conditions and illnesses.

Regular wellness vet visits will help ensure that your Greyhound stays fit and happy.

Corns

If your Greyhound limps and has a hard, somewhat circular and whitish area on one of his toe pads, he has a corn. This is a "Greyhound thing." Corns extend deep into the pad and are always painful, so if your boy has a corn, he'll want to walk on grass and carpet and avoid pavement or flooring. Treatment options are many, and treatment is often effective. But a corn that seems to no longer exist may reappear. When a corn isn't amenable to treatment, maintenance is required to help the dog walk as painlessly as possible. Your vet might recommend Thera-Paw boots, which have been found by many Greyhound owners to make

a big difference in their dog's comfort. Thera-Paw boots are also helpful for injured or torn nails, including those from symmetrical lupoid onychodystrophy (SLO), described later in this chapter. If your dog is a strong chewer or chews when he is bored, don't leave the boot on when he's alone—or have him wear a cone so that he can't chew the boot.

Amputation of the affected digit is the course of last resort in treatment of a corn, but it doesn't prevent another corn from appearing elsewhere.

Lumbosacral Stenosis (LS)

Greyhounds aren't prone to hip dysplasia, which affects so many other large breeds, but in their later years they're prone to another disorder that makes dogs weak in the hind end: lumbosacral stenosis (LS). LS makes the last part of the dog's spinal canal become narrowed, causing the nerve roots to compress. Lameness, wobbliness, dragging one foot, difficulty getting up from the floor, and rear-end pain signal LS in older Greys, especially males. There is effective treatment, but LS can be difficult to diagnose for the vet who isn't familiar with it.

Osteosarcoma (OSA)

All dogs can get cancer, and Greyhounds in their senior years are prone to a primary bone tumor called osteosarcoma. Most often it occurs in a leg or shoulder, with symptoms being swelling, limping, or spontaneous fracture (a bone breaking for no apparent reason). Amputation of the affected limb followed by chemotherapy offers an average survival time of about a year. Amputation alone won't increase survival time following diagnosis, which is about four months, but it ends the severe pain of OSA. Greyhounds tend to do well on just three legs, and usually the side effects of chemotherapy are minimal. But whether to amputate or not is a decision that only a dog's owner should make. It isn't cruel to amputate. Nor is it cruel to euthanize. Both are acts of love.

Pannus

Pannus, or chronic superficial keratitis, is a disorder of the immune system that affects a dog's eyes. Essentially, the immune system decides that the eye is foreign tissue and attacks it. The root cause may be infection or injury. Early symptoms are redness and sensitivity. Sunlight is known to worsen the condition. If your dog's eyes look red or he rubs them continually, take him to the vet. Pannus is treated with cortisone drops or injections of cortisone under the outer surface of the eye. As yet there is no cure, but the disease can usually be controlled without discomfort to the dog or loss of vision.

Symmetrical Lupoid Onychodystrophy (SLO)

Also called pemphigus, SLO is another autoimmune condition, and it causes Greyhounds to lose multiple nails. Additional symptoms may include nail licking, oozing around the base of the nail, separation of the nail from the quick, limping, infection, and odor. A vet not familiar with SLO may confuse it with a fungal or bacterial infection and want to amputate the tip of a toe to make a diagnosis. This surgery is unnecessary. If your vet isn't a Greyhound specialist, you can provide her with information on SLO and its treatment.

General Illnesses

Dogs of all types are subject to a wide variety of diseases and disorders, just as we are. This is why we watch for changes in our dogs and give them timely veterinary care. Here are some illnesses that Greyhounds are not predisposed to but may get.

Allergies

Dogs, like humans, can develop allergies to any number of things found in foods, household products, and the very air we breathe. Allergic inhalant dermatitis, or atopy, is a reaction to something inhaled, such as pollen, dust mites, mold, or feathers. Even human dander can cause a reaction in dogs (and we thought it was the other way around). Your dog can also be allergic to the food you put in his bowl or just possibly the bowl itself. Flea saliva is a common cause of allergic reaction. There are contact allergies, such as to grass and other plants.

Like humans, dogs can develop allergies to things like grasses.

The excessive licking, chewing, or scratching at the skin that dogs do when they suffer from allergies can have harmful effects. Your vet can conduct skin testing to try to find the source of your dog's problem and can give him medication to make him more comfortable. She may also have him wear an Elizabethan collar, a head cover available in clear plastic or soft fabric. Also called a "cone" or "E-collar," it prevents the dog from bothering a wound or an itch from allergies. In my house, the cone is called a Happy Hat because each

GASTRIC DILATATION VOLVULUS (GDV)

—Rodger Barr, DVM

Gastric dilatation volvulus (GDV), also called torsion or bloat, is a threat to all dog breeds. However, "bloat" is not an accurate term for this condition; it suggests that the problem is just an accumulation of air, fluid, or food in the stomach, when actually it is a filling and twisting of the stomach and adjacent structures. Thus, "torsion" should be added to the phrase.

Are Greyhounds predisposed to bloat? The incidence doesn't seem to be greater than in any other large deep-chested breed, and if the truth be known, much less often than they are given credit for. I have cared for many Greyhounds over the past 34 years and to date have experienced only five cases. GDV appears to be more prevalent in AKC Greyhounds than racers, possibly due to their extremely deep chests. Post-surgical bloat is quite common. The type of surgery seems not to matter. The bottom line is yes, the problem does occur, but I don't believe the frequency to be excessively high in Greyhounds.

The most frequent symptom of bloat is dry heaves, attempts at vomiting that are, for the most part, nonproductive. The second most frequently seen symptom is an enlarged abdomen. As owners of a shorthaired dog, we are able to recognize this sooner than owners of longhaired breeds. Once symptoms are suspected, seek professional help immediately. If quickly diagnosed and rectified, there will be less chance of complications. Surgical intervention is frequently required but not always. If an exploratory procedure is initiated to resolve the condition, the surgeon is able to perform a permanent procedure to prevent subsequent GDV episodes; this procedure is called a gastropexy.

Several precautionary practices should be adhered to. Avoiding exercise before feeding is of limited value, except that an exhausted dog should not be fed and should be given water at a reasonably slow rate. It helps immensely to feed at least two meals a day, which means all meals will be smaller in size. The critical precaution is to avoid excessive exercise for at least two hours following a meal so that the food can be digested and leave the stomach. Also, avoid walks after feeding. The rhythmic effect of a slow walk on a full stomach can cause a progressively pendulum-like swing that is capable of flipping. Lastly, if your pet is prone to lying on his back after dinner, do what you can to discourage this adorable but risky habit, as abnormal positioning can occur.

Recent research suggests that raised feeders contribute to bloat by causing excessive swallowing of air, which contributes to gastric inflation. Greyhounds with bad necks should be fed from a raised feeder, but once their neck issues are resolved, ground-level feeding should be resumed.

My suggestions for all of you who share your lives with these wonderful animals is to enjoy them and don't live in fear of bloat. Consider the suggestions presented above, but don't lose sleep over this condition. There are other dog owners who have more to worry about than you do.

time it's slipped over the dog's head, a liver treat is given. You'll want to remove the cone for walks, potty breaks, and feeding.

Gastric Dilatation Volvulus (GDV)

Gastric dilatation volvulus, commonly called "bloat" or "stomach torsion," is an extremely serious disorder. When a dog bloats, his stomach fills with air and becomes twisted to the point that he may go into shock and die. The most frequent symptoms are unsuccessful attempts to vomit and an enlarged abdomen. There's nothing you can do to reduce the symptoms, so seek professional help immediately. Phone your vet to say that you are bringing in a dog who appears to be bloating. If you suspect bloat at a time when your vet's office is closed, take your dog to the nearest animal emergency hospital, phoning first if possible. Even if the stomach hasn't yet rotated, GDV is life threatening.

At most risk for bloat are large dogs ages five and up who have deep and narrow chests. Also at risk are dogs with a first-degree relative who has had bloat and dogs who wolf their food. Ways to reduce the risk include feeding small meals two or three times a day instead of one large meal and feeding a food gulper from a large cookie sheet rather than a bowl. The best prevention, though, is to restrict exercise before and after eating—with

after being the most crucial. (See sidebar "Gastric Dilatation Volvulus [GDV].")

Heatstroke

Heatstroke is a life-threatening condition caused by prolonged exposure to hot sun or being in an enclosed area that is too warm and poorly ventilated. Because Greyhounds lack the insulation of a thick coat, they overheat quickly, especially those with dark hair. Dogs don't sweat when they're hot; they pant, so hard panting on a hot day is cause for alarm. As measures you can take to cool an overheated dog before you can get him to the vet, the American Kennel Club (AKC) recommends offering a small amount of water to drink, ice chips to lick, and Pedialyte to restore electrolytes; hosing him down with cool water; applying an ice pack to the groin area; and rubbing alcohol to the paw pads. If you aren't certain that he's in danger, assume that he is and take action. The point is that if your dog really does have heatstroke, you must act swiftly. The car ride to the vet comes immediately after you've cooled your dog down as best you can.

Never exercise your dog outdoors on a hot day or leave him in the car, even on a day that's only slightly warm, with the windows closed or only partially open, as the temperature inside the car will far exceed the temperature outside. And never leave him in a doghouse—which

Never exercise your Greyhound outdoors on a hot day or he could experience heatstroke.

you shouldn't have for a Greyhound—or in the garage.

There is a rumor passed around via e-mail that one should never, under any circumstances, give dogs iced or very cold water. The reasoning in this rumor, which is refuted on many Internet sites, is that doing so can cause the dog to bloat. Dr. Rodger Barr, a veterinarian specializing in sighthounds, says that "Under normal circumstances, cold water or ice cubes will cause no problems for dogs. However, dogs who are overheated or who have exercised hard should have regulated water consumption because drinking too much too rapidly is counterproductive and may cause vomiting." Dr. Barr recommends cooling the dog down with cold water on the head

and feet as well as the body (including the underside). Water consumption is also recommended—just not too much and not too cold.

Hypothyroidism

Hypothyroidism, a deficiency of the T4 hormone (produced by the thyroid gland), is common to dogs and humans and can lead to obesity, lethargy, mental dullness, poor skin, and hair loss. Less commonly, muscles and nerves are affected. In dogs it's most frequently seen in middle-aged females. Accurate diagnosis is important because treating a dog for hypothyroidism when it doesn't exist may disrupt hormonal balance.

Hypothyroidism is treated with oral administration of thyroid hormone

(T4). Make sure that your vet knows that Greyhounds normally have only half as much T4 as other breeds, that their heart rate is slower, and that bald thighs in a Greyhound don't signal the disease. The cause of bald-thigh syndrome is actually unknown, and bald thighs are seen in dogs with low, high, and normal thyroid levels.

The best resource for information on hypothyroidism is www.greyhealth.com, an archive of Dr. Suzanne Stack's articles on Greyhound health.

Impacted Anal Sacs

Your Greyhound, like other predators, has two anal sacs located just below his anus. The sacs, also called "anal glands," are filled with a musky fluid that identifies him to other dogs and is emptied with every bowel movement. This way of saying "I was here!" is why other dogs like to sniff your dog's poop and he likes to sniff theirs. When anal glands don't empty properly, they can become impacted, which can lead to infection. If your dog persistently licks his anus or "scoots" around on his fanny, take him to the vet to have his anal sacs expressed. The doctor can teach you how to do this at home—if you're so inclined.

Pancreatitis

Pancreatitis is an inflammatory disease of the pancreas, a small gland that sits beside the small intestine in the abdomen and keeps busy by manufacturing and secreting digestive enzymes and insulin. Signs of pancreatitis may include loss of appetite, lethargy, fever, vomiting, diarrhea, and a painful abdomen. Many dogs with pancreatitis are overweight, but a dog can get pancreatitis from eating just one high-fat meal (no bacon fat, please!). Another common cause is trauma or injury that involves the abdomen. Treatment involves no oral intake, including water, in order to reduce pancreatic stimulation. Intravenous fluids will be given until vomiting has stopped and the dog can keep food and water down. Antibiotics and anti-vomit medicines are usually needed.

Reverse Sneezing

Reverse sneezing, also known as paroxysmal respiration or pharyngeal gag reflex, is a canine condition caused by irritation of the soft palate. It isn't actually sneezing but a spasm in which the dog gasps inward—making him look as if he's having trouble breathing. The condition is more common in short-faced breeds such as Boxers and Pugs, but any breed can experience it, and many Greyhounds do.

Some dogs have episodes of reverse sneezing their entire lives, but most develop the problem with age. During a spasm, the dog will extend his neck while making a loud snorting sound. He may turn his elbows, and his eyes may bulge while his chest expands as he tries harder to inhale. All of this adds to the owner's fear that something terrible is taking place. Actually, the dog's trachea has become narrow, and it is harder to get a normal amount of air into the lungs. But episodes are brief—one or two minutes, maybe less—and there are no aftereffects. You can help with a gentle massage of his throat and soothing words. However, if reverse sneezing is a continuing condition and episodes become more severe or more frequent, schedule an examination of his nasal passages and throat. Sinusitis or another respiratory disorder may be the root cause. If allergies are the problem, your vet will prescribe antihistamines.

Parasites

Parasites are tiny animals that at some point in their life cycle depend on a host—such as your dog—for sustenance. While not all parasites are harmful, the ones discussed in this section are.

External Parasites

External parasites are those that remain mostly outside the dog's body while feeding.

Fleas

Fleas can be a year-round problem in warm climates, but in cold climates they're usually seen only during the warm months. During flea season, check for fleas daily, even if they're uncommon in your area, and have a flea comb on hand in case the need for one arises. Fleas can live anywhere on your dog and are so small that they can hide out in the short, fine hair of a Greyhound. Examine your dog everywhere, especially around the eyes, ears, and base of his tail, and even between his toes. If you find shiny black specks the size of coal dust on your dog and they turn reddish-brown on a piece of wet paper, they are flea droppings of digested blood. (You're right—*ugh!*) Use your flea comb to catch fleas (or ticks) that are on your dog but not attached to him, then quickly dunk the comb in a bowl of soapsudsy warm water or rubbing alcohol to drown them.

Never use a flea collar—or any other flea product that comes in contact with your Greyhound's skin—that has permethrin on the label. Commonly found in flea collars and commercial flea preventives, permethrin is so dangerous for sighthounds that it can cause death. Your veterinarian may suggest a topical flea preventive containing pyrethrins, which are derived from plants and are safe for your dog. Man-made equivalents of pyrethrins are called pyrethroids, and these too are safe. But with so many flea products out there, it can be confusing. Just remember these three things: Permethrin is not safe for your Greyhound, products that are safe for

FIRST-AID KIT

Have a doggy first-aid kit handy for home use and keep perishables in it up to date. Items to include are:

- antibacterial ointment
- antidiarrheal (ask your vet's advice)
- Benadryl (for allergic reactions)
- bulb syringe or medicine syringe
- canine first-aid manual
- cotton balls
- ear wash
- EMT gel and/or spray
- flashlight
- gauze bandages
- ice pack
- hydrocortisone cream
- hydrogen peroxide in 3% solution (USP)
- muzzle
- Neosporin
- Pepto-Bismol
- petroleum jelly for sore paws
- styptic powder for cracked or broken nails
- rabies certificate
- rectal thermometer
- saline eye solution to flush eyes
- scissors
- splints
- telephone numbers for your vet, the nearest animal emergency hospital, a friend or neighbor who can help, your adoption group, and the National Animal Poison Control Center (NAPCC)—1-888-4ANI-HELP or 1-900-443-0000
- topical antibiotic
- tweezers
- vet wrap (self-adhering bandages)

puppies and kittens generally are safe for Greys, and you can rely on the advice of your veterinarian.

More bad news about fleas: They hop around and get into carpets and rugs and bedding (not just your dog's but yours too). So if there are fleas in the house, machine wash and dry all bedding—and vacuum with a vengeance. To prevent flea larvae from hiding and maturing, cover both your dog's favorite sleeping areas and upholstered furniture with cotton sheets, and every week of flea season roll the sheets up to be laundered in hot water. If you have a serious infestation, talk to your vet before taking action with a pesticide "bomb" to rid your home of the fleas.

Ticks

Ticks are even nastier than fleas, as they transmit the widest variety of pathogens of all bloodsucking arthropods. Of the deadly diseases that ticks inflict on animals and humans, perhaps the one most people are familiar with is Lyme disease. But the others are just as serious.

Check your Greyhound for fleas and ticks after he's been playing outdoors.

Any Greyhound bred for racing may have lived with Greyhounds from parts of the country where tick-borne diseases are endemic, and some of them can lie dormant for years before causing illness. Ehrlichiosis, for instance, can remain dormant for up to seven years before showing symptoms. No matter where you live, your dog may have been infected prior to adoption, and your vet should know this.

The only good news about ticks is that they don't jump or hop from one place to another. They're crawlers, and they wait—on tall grasses, leaves, and even lawns only a few inches (cm) high—for their food source to brush against them, which is when they move from plant to animal. On park walks, your Greyhound will probably want to sniff, raise his leg, or brush up against tall grasses. As much as you want him to enjoy life, try not to indulge this desire. And check your dog and yourself for ticks after each outing to somewhere that ticks may be encountered.

To remove an attached tick, grasp it with tweezers or a tick remover as close to where it's attached to the dog as you can, and slowly pull it straight out. Don't twist as you pull, or the mouth parts will stay buried in your dog's skin and can cause infection. Put the tick into alcohol or flush it down the toilet. Ticks are hard to kill and live for years, so don't throw it in the trash unless you're certain that it's dead.

Many veterinarians and Greyhound adoption groups recommend a Greyhound-safe flea and tick preventive that you apply topically between your dog's shoulder blades. This kills ticks before they have a chance to transmit disease. Given that transmission of the tick-borne disease anaplasmosis can occur in as short a time as four hours, I can't imagine not protecting my Greyhounds from ticks this way. Use the preventive only as directed by your vet.

Mange

Mange is an all-inclusive word for several skin disorders caused by different species of arachnids called mites. Mange is characterized by hair loss, severe itching, crusty and irritated skin, lesions at the ear tips, or a moth-eaten appearance anywhere on the dog. Although mange is not commonplace in healthy dogs living in clean conditions, sarcoptic mange (also called scabies) is highly contagious, and demodectic mange (or demodex) can be passed from mother to puppy—even if the mom hasn't shown symptoms. If you suspect mange, see your vet.

Ringworm

Ringworm is actually a fungus, not a worm. It grows on the skin, causing hair loss (often a raw-looking bald patch) and itching. Diagnosis is made by examining the skin using a black light. Ringworm is contagious and can spread to humans. Don't try to treat this yourself. See your vet—she will prescribe medication.

Internal Parasites

Internal parasites found in dogs range from harmless to deadly. Here are some that you and your vet will want to guard your Greyhound against.

Heartworms

Heartworm disease, which is found throughout the United States, is spread by mosquitoes carrying the worm's larvae. Heartworm is so named because it invades the host animal's heart. The damage it does is gradual, but the end result is congestive heart failure. Heartworm is detected by a blood test, and you never want the heartbreak of having it found in your dog. If caught early, there is treatment, but it's very hard on the dog. There are Greyhound-safe heartworm preventives that are given monthly and provide complete protection.

Hookworms

Hookworms attach to a dog's intestines and feed on his blood. In large numbers

HEALTH CHECKLIST

✓ Choose a vet who either has knowledge of the Greyhound's anatomical differences or is willing to consult with a vet who does.
✓ Schedule annual examinations.
✓ Keep up to date with vaccinations.
✓ If your dog displays symptoms of illness or if you sense that something is amiss, take him to the vet.
✓ Guard against your Greyhound's becoming overheated, and know what to do if it happens.
✓ Protect your dog against parasites by using Greyhound-safe preventives.

they can cause anemia and digestive disorders, especially in puppies. The presence of hookworms is found by examination of a stool specimen.

Good news: Your Greyhound's monthly heartworm preventive will also prevent hookworms.

Roundworms

Roundworms infest the small intestine, causing malnourishment and sometimes anemia and pneumonia. A mother dog who has been infested at any time in her life can transmit roundworms to her puppies during gestation or nursing. The worms, which resemble strings of spaghetti, show up in feces and vomit. This too can be controlled by a heartworm preventive.

Whipworms

Whipworms infest the large intestine and appendix, causing digestive disorders that can lead to bacterial infection.

Resembling bits of thread, whipworms are both hard to diagnose and eradicate. When a retired racer has had diarrhea since leaving the track and has tested negative for worms in a fecal exam, it's strongly recommended that he be dewormed with Panacur (check with your vet) before any further diagnostics are done. This can save the Greyhound unnecessary distress and save his owner a bundle that she didn't need to spend.

Surgery

Greyhound owners rightfully worry about their dogs being anesthetized, as anesthesia protocols tolerated by other dogs have historically been a problem for Greys. Fortunately, the situation has improved. Barbiturates, the main culprit in unnecessary deaths from anesthesia, have given way to new and safer anesthetics. Even so, when a surgical procedure is necessary, it's best to take your dog to a vet with experience

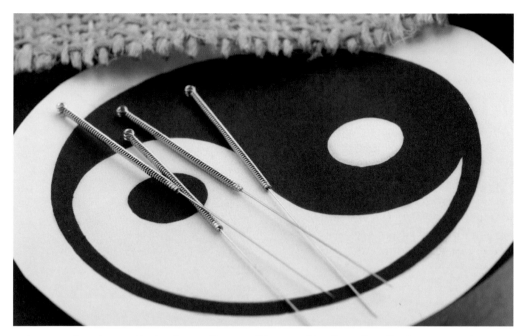

Acupuncture is used to treat specific conditions and to strengthen the immune system.

in anesthetizing Greyhounds. If this isn't possible, have her consult with a Greyhound specialist. A good choice would be the vet used by your adoption group when new dogs come off the track. Whomever you go to, make sure that monitoring of your dog throughout the entire procedure will be done by a vet tech. Electronic monitoring is a plus but doesn't take the place of a skilled person.

Alternative Therapies

Nontraditional veterinary care goes by several synonymous names: alternative, complementary, holistic, and integrative.

As in traditional medicine, alternative medicine includes a number of fields in which a vet may specialize. Alternative care for both humans and animals has been a growing phenomenon in Western countries for decades; in the East, it's been around for thousands of years. Just a few of the many modalities available are described in this section. Choose a holistic practitioner the same way you would choose a traditional doctor for your dog: Get referrals, do research, and only see licensed professionals. Keep in mind, too, that just like traditional medications, herbs and supplements can have side effects.

Acupuncture

Acupuncture involves sticking very small needles into specific points in the body to improve energy flow. Used in China for 3,500 years, it is the main treatment of a quarter of the world's population. In veterinary care, acupuncture is used to treat specific conditions and to strengthen the body's immune system. For more information, visit the website of the American Academy of Veterinary Acupuncture (AAVA) at www.aava.org.

Chiropractic

Used to treat many conditions, chiropractic identifies and corrects misaligned or fixated vertebrae (series of small bones forming the spine) through hands-on adjustments. For more information, visit the website of the American Veterinary Chiropractic Association (AVCA) at www. animalchiropractic.org.

Herbal Therapy

The goal of herbal therapy is to help the body heal itself by boosting the immune system. An herbalist in the Chinese tradition makes a customized blend of herbs to promote well-being or balance in the body. In the Western (or European) tradition, a specific herb is used to treat a specific ailment. Consult with your regular vet before starting your dog on herbal therapy. For more information, visit

The goal of herbal therapy is to help the body heal itself by boosting the immune system.

the website of the Veterinary Botanical Medical Association (VBMA) at www. vbma.org.

Homeopathy

Homeopathy dates back to Hippocrates and works on the principle of "*Similia similibus curentur*," or "like cures like." Homeopathic remedics are made from substances that in large doses can cause illness and are administered in diluted, minute doses to effect a cure. For more information, visit the website of the American Holistic Veterinary Medical Association (AHVMA) at www.ahvma.org.

The Senior Greyhound

A Greyhound enters his senior years at age seven. No matter how healthy your dog is, watch for signs of possible problems. Increased thirst, more frequent urination or bowel movements, a change in eating habits, or lethargy should be reported to his vet. Old dogs of any breed can develop canine cognitive dysfunction syndrome (CDS), often called doggy Alzheimer's. Among the many symptoms are aimless wandering, confusion, and staring at walls. There is an FDA-approved medication for the treatment of CDS.

Euthanasia

None of us wants to think about euthanasia. But except for the dog who perishes in an accident or dies in his sleep, our beloved canine companions are gently put to rest by their veterinarian—while we, our hearts breaking, hold them in our arms or lie next to them. The process, which your vet will explain to you, is virtually painless. Sedation is brought about by injection, followed after your dog is asleep by a second injection that causes the heart to stop. It is over in a few seconds. Not the love, though. A dog's time in this world is brief, but his time in your heart is forever. What better tribute to your Greyhound than to protect him from needless suffering, grieve for him when he goes, and—when you are ready—adopt another Greyhound.

As a new member of the ever-growing and deeply caring community of Greyhound lovers, you will hear divergent opinions on what is best for your dog: Crate; don't crate. Let the dog run in a fenced yard; he shouldn't run—it's dangerous. Feed raw; feed top-quality dog food. Allow him on furniture so that he'll be happy; he'll be better behaved if not allowed on furniture.

The list of what we agree to disagree on is long, but on this we all agree: A Greyhound should never be off leash except in a completely enclosed area. Lord Tennyson wrote of "greyhounds fleeting like a beam of light." Allow your Greyhound to run free and the time it takes him to disappear may be as fleeting as a beam of light. Our job as Greyhound owners is to do everything within our power to keep our dogs happy, healthy, and safe. If at the end of the day you can say that you've done this, you will be the best thing that ever happened to your dog. He is on earth solely to be your companion and loved by you.

Congratulations and welcome to the worldwide Greyhound community!

Resources

Associations and Organizations

Breed Clubs

American Kennel Club (AKC)
5580 Centerview Drive
Raleigh, NC 27606
Telephone: (919) 233-9767
Fax: (919) 233-3627
E-Mail: info@akc.org
www.akc.org

Canadian Kennel Club (CKC)
89 Skyway Avenue, Suite 100
Etobicoke, Ontario M9W 6R4
Telephone: (416) 675-5511
Fax: (416) 675-6506
E-Mail: information@ckc.ca
www.ckc.ca

Federation Cynologique Internationale (FCI)
Secretariat General de la FCI
Place Albert 1er, 13
B – 6530 Thuin
Belqique
www.fci.be

Greyhound Club of America (GCA)
www.greyhoundclubofamerica.org

Greyhound Club of Canada (GCC)
R R 2 C/O Laurie Soutar
Princeton
Province ON
Postal Code N0J 1V0
Telephone: (519) 458-8429

The Kennel Club
1 Clarges Street
London
W1J 8AB
Telephone: 0870 606 6750
Fax: 0207 518 1058
www.the-kennel-club.org.uk

National Greyhound Association (NGA)
P.O. Box 543
Abilene, KS 67410
Telephone: (785) 263-4660
E-Mail: nga@ngagreyhounds.com
www.ngagreyhounds.com

United Kennel Club (UKC)
100 E. Kilgore Road
Kalamazoo, MI 49002-5584
Telephone: (269) 343-9020
Fax: (269) 343-7037
E-Mail: pbickell@ukcdogs.com
www.ukcdogs.com

Pet Sitters

National Association of Professional Pet Sitters
15000 Commerce Parkway, Suite C
Mt. Laurel, New Jersey 08054
Telephone: (856) 439-0324
Fax: (856) 439-0525
E-Mail: napps@ahint.com
www.petsitters.org

Pet Sitters International
201 East King Street
King, NC 27021-9161
Telephone: (336) 983-9222
Fax: (336) 983-5266
E-Mail: info@petsit.com
www.petsit.com

Rescue Organizations and Animal Welfare Groups

American Humane Association (AHA)
63 Inverness Drive East
Englewood, CO 80112
Telephone: (303) 792-9900
Fax: 792-5333
www.americanhumane.org

American Society for the Prevention of Cruelty to Animals (ASPCA)
424 E. 92nd Street
New York, NY 10128-6804
Telephone: (212) 876-7700
www.aspca.org

The Greyhound Project, Inc.
P.O. Box 5239
Framingham, MA 01701
Telephone: (617) 527-8843
www.adopt-a-greyhound.org

The Humane Society of the United States
(HSUS)
2100 L Street, NW
Washington DC 20037
Telephone: (202) 452-1100
www.hsus.org

Royal Society for the Prevention of Cruelty to
Animals (RSPCA)
RSPCA Enquiries Service
Wilberforce Way, Southwater,
Horsham, West Sussex RH13 9RS
United Kingdom
Telephone: 0870 3335 999
Fax: 0870 7530 284
www.rspca.org.uk

Sports
International Agility Link (IAL)
Global Administrator: Steve Drinkwater
E-Mail: yunde@powerup.au
www.agilityclick.com/~ial

The World Canine Freestyle Organization, Inc.
P.O. Box 350122
Brooklyn, NY 11235
Telephone: (718) 332-8336
Fax: (718) 646-2686
E-Mail: WCFODOGS@aol.com
www.worldcaninefreestyle.org

Therapy
Delta Society
875 124th Ave, NE, Suite 101
Bellevue, WA 98005
Telephone: (425) 679-5500
Fax: (425) 679-5539
E-Mail: info@DeltaSociety.org
www.deltasociety.org

Therapy Dogs Inc.
P.O. Box 20227
Cheyenne WY 82003
Telephone: (877) 843-7364
Fax: (307) 638-2079
E-Mail: therapydogsinc@qwestoffice.net
www.therapydogs.com

Therapy Dogs International (TDI)
88 Bartley Road
Flanders, NJ 07836
Telephone: (973) 252-9800
Fax: (973) 252-7171
E-Mail: tdi@gti.net
www.tdi-dog.org

Training
Association of Pet Dog Trainers (APDT)
150 Executive Center Drive Box 35
Greenville, SC 29615
Telephone: (800) PET-DOGS
Fax: (864) 331-0767
E-Mail: information@apdt.com
www.apdt.com

International Association of Animal Behavior
Consultants (IAABC)
565 Callery Road
Cranberry Township, PA 16066
E-Mail: info@iaabc.org
www.iaabc.org

National Association of Dog Obedience
Instructors (NADOI)
PMB 369
729 Grapevine Hwy.
Hurst, TX 76054-2085
www.nadoi.org

Veterinary and Health Resources
Academy of Veterinary Homeopathy (AVH)
P.O. Box 9280
Wilmington, DE 19809
Telephone: (866) 652-1590
Fax: (866) 652-1590
www.theavh.org

American Academy of Veterinary Acupuncture
(AAVA)
P.O. Box 1058
Glastonbury, CT 06033
Telephone: (860) 632-9911
Fax: (860) 659-8772
www.aava.org

American Animal Hospital Association (AAHA)
12575 W. Bayaud Ave.
Lakewood, CO 80228
Telephone: (303) 986-2800
Fax: (303) 986-1700
E-Mail: info@aahanet.org
www.aahanet.org/index.cfm

American College of Veterinary Internal Medicine (ACVIM)
1997 Wadsworth Blvd., Suite A
Lakewood, CO 80214-5293
Telephone: (800) 245-9081
Fax: (303) 231-0880
Email: ACVIM@ACVIM.org
www.acvim.org

American College of Veterinary Ophthalmologists (ACVO)
P.O. Box 1311
Meridian, ID 83860
Telephone: (208) 466-7624
Fax: (208) 466-7693
E-Mail: office09@acvo.com
www.acvo.com

American Holistic Veterinary Medical Association (AHVMA)
2218 Old Emmorton Road
Bel Air, MD 21015
Telephone: (410) 569-0795
Fax: (410) 569-2346
E-Mail: office@ahvma.org
www.ahvma.org

American Veterinary Medical Association (AVMA)
1931 North Meacham Road, Suite 100
Schaumburg, IL 60173-4360
Telephone: (847) 925-8070
Fax: (847) 925-1329
E-Mail: avmainfo@avma.org
www.avma.org

ASPCA Animal Poison Control Center
Telephone: (888) 426-4435
www.aspca.org

British Veterinary Association (BVA)
7 Mansfield Street
London
W1G 9NQ
Telephone: 0207 636 6541
Fax: 0207 908 6349
E-Mail: bvahq@bva.co.uk
www.bva.co.uk

Canine Eye Registration Foundation (CERF)
VMDB/CERF
1717 Philo Rd
P O Box 3007
Urbana, IL 61803-3007
Telephone: (217) 693-4800
Fax: (217) 693-4801
E-Mail: CERF@vmbd.org
www.vmdb.org

Grassmere Animal Hospital
3926 Nolensville Road
Nashville, TN 37211
Telephone: (615) 832-6535
www.grassmere-animal-hospital.com/
greyhounds.htm

Greyt Health
Archived Articles on Greyhound Health
Suzanne Stack, DVM
E-Mail: Yumadons@gmail.com
www.greythealth.com

Ohio State University Greyhound Health and Wellness Program
601 Vernon L. Tharp Street
Columbus, OH 43210
Telephone: (614) 292-3551
E-Mail: couto.1@osu.edu
http://vet.osu.edu/hospital

Orthopedic Foundation for Animals (OFA)
2300 NE Nifong Blvd
Columbus, Missouri 65201-3856
Telephone: (573) 442-0418
Fax: (573) 875-5073
Email: ofa@offa.org
www.offa.org

University of Illinois College of Veterinary Medicine, Office of Public Engagement
2001 S. Lincoln Avenue
Urbana, IL 61802-6199
Telephone: (217) 333-2907
http://www.cvm.uiuc.edu

US Food and Drug Administration Center for Veterinary Medicine (CVM)
7519 Standish Place
HFV-12
Rockville, MD 20855-0001
Telephone: (240) 276-9300 or (888) INFO-FDA
http://www.fda.gov/cvm

Publications
Books

Branigan, Cynthia A. *Adopting the Racing Greyhound.* Howell Book House, 2003.

Caras, Roger A. *A Dog Is Listening: The Way Some of Our Closest Friends View Us.* Fireside, 1998.

Coile, Caroline D., Ph.D. *Greyhounds: A Complete Pet Owner's Manual.* Barron's, 2001.

Comfort, David. *The First Pet History of the World.* Simon & Schuster, Inc.,1994. (currently out of print)

Finch, Anne. *Pet Owner's Guide to the Greyhound.* Ringpress Books, 2000.

Fox, Dr. Michael W. *The Healing Touch for Dogs: The Proven Massage Program for Dogs.* Newmarket Press, 2004.

Fox, Dr. Michael W., Elizabeth Hodgkins, and Marion E. Smart. *Not Fit for a Dog!: The Truth About Manufactured Dog and Cat Food.* Quill Driver Books, 2008.

Lackey, Sue A. *Greyhounds in America: A Comprehensive Record of the Breed, Vol. 1, Presented by The Greyhound Club of America, Inc., 1989.* (currently out of print)

Livingood, Lee. *Retired Racing Greyhounds for Dummies.* For Dummies, 2000.

Nourissier, François, and Elisabeth Foucart-Walter. *Dogs in the Louvre.* Flammarion, 2008.

Magazines

AKC Family Dog
American Kennel Club
260 Madison Avenue
New York, NY 10016
Telephone: (800) 490-5675
E-Mail: familydog@akc.org
www.akc.org/pubs/familydog

AKC Gazette
American Kennel Club
260 Madison Avenue
New York, NY 10016
Telephone: (800) 533-7323
E-Mail: gazette@akc.org
www.akc.org/pubs/gazette

Celebrating Greyhounds Magazine
P.O. Box 5239
Framingham, MA 01701
E-Mail: subscriptions@adopt-a-greyhound.org
www.adopt-a-greyhound.org/cgmagazine

Dog & Kennel
Pet Publishing, Inc.
7-L Dundas Circle
Greensboro, NC 27407
Telephone: (336) 292-4272
Fax: (336) 292-4272
E-Mail: info@petpublishing.com
www.dogandkennel.com

Dogs Monthly
Ascot House
High Street, Ascot,
Berkshire SL5 7JG
United Kingdom
Telephone: 0870 730 8433
Fax: 0870 730 8431
E-Mail: admin@rtc-associates.freeserve.co.uk
www.corsini.co.uk/dogsmonthly

Greyhounds Magazine
Dog Fancy: Popular Dog Series
P.O. Box 53264
Boulder, CO 80322-3264
Telephone: (800) 365-4421
E-Mail: barkback@dogfancy.com
www.dogfancy.com

Websites

Dr. Michael W. Fox
www.twobitdog.com/DrFox

Nylabone
www.nylabone.com

TFH Publications, Inc.
www.tfh.com

Index

Note: Boldfaced numbers indicate illustrations.

cognitive dysfunction syndrome, 94, 133
corns, 119
distemper, 118
external parasites, 126–129
gastric dilatation volvulus, 122–123
heatstroke, 14, 123–124,
hepatitis, 118
hypothyroidism, 124–125
impacted anal sacs, 125
internal parasites, 129–130
kennel cough, 118
leptospirosis, 118
lumbosacral stenosis, 119–120
Lyme disease, 118
osteosarcoma, 120
pancreatitis, 125
pannus, 120
parainfluenza, 118
paroxysmal respiration, 125–126
pharyngeal gag reflex, 125–126
reverse sneezing, 125–126
stomach torsion, 122–123
symmetrical lupoid onychodystropy, 119–121
impacted anal sacs, 125
International Association of Animal Behavior Consultants (IAABC), 20, 135

J
jumping behavior, 94–95

K
Kennel Club (KC), 8, 100, 134
kennel cough (bordetella), 118
kibble (dry dog food), 45–47

L
Large Gazehound Racing Association (LGRA), 102–103
leads/leashes
   defined, 30
   introducing forever home, 86
   recommendations, 35
   for safety, 22
   when house training, 78
legs and feet
   breed characteristics, 19–22
   corns, 119
   SLO condition, 119–121

leptospirosis, 118

life expectancy, 25, 133
literature, Greyhounds in, 10–11
Livingood, Lee, 20, 73, 88
living with Greyhounds
   companionability, 22
   daily schedules, 22, 31
   environment, 22–23
   exercise requirements, 23–24
   health. See health care
   life expectancy, 25
   sensitive nature, 22,
   trainability, 25
   watchdog ability, 25
lost/loose Greyhounds, 36–38, 90
lumbosacral stenosis (LS), 119–120
lure coursing, 10, 101–104
Lyme disease, 118

M
mange, 129
marking behavior, 94–95
martingale collars, 30–31
meet and greets, 105–106
microchips, 35
mites, 129
muzzles, 35–36,

N
nail care, 34, 62–65
National Greyhound Association (NGA), 36, 134
National Oval Track Racing Association (NOTRA), 103
neck characteristics, 19
neutering, 117
nitting behavior, 95–96
noises, handling, 87
noncommercial dog foods, 47–48
nutrition considerations. See feeding Greyhounds
Nylabone chews
   chewing behavior and, 91
   crate training and, 76
   resource information, 137
   size considerations, 39
   table manners and, 55

O
obedience commands. See commands
obesity, 54
off command, 88, 90, 93
omega-3 fatty acids, 48–49
osteosarcoma (OSA), 120

P
pajamas, 28–29
pancreatitis, 125
pannus (chronic superficial keratitis), 120
parainfluenza, 118
parasites
   external, 126–129
   internal, 129–130
paroxysmal respiration, 125–126
pemphigus (SLO), 119–121
periodontal disease, 67
pet insurance, 116–117
pet sitters, 134
pharyngeal gag reflex, 125–126
positive training, 72,
prison foster programs, 9–10
problem solving. *See also* training Greyhounds
   adjusting to forever home, 86–89
   aggression and separation anxiety, 92
   barking behavior, 90–91
   biting behavior, 92
   checklist for, 94
   chewing behavior, 91–92
   counter surfing, 92–93
   digging behavior, 93
   finding behaviorists, 97
   growling behavior, 92
   guarding possessions, 92
   health problems, 116
   house soiling, 93–94
   jumping behavior, 94–95
   loose Greyhounds, 90
   marking behavior, 94–95
   nitting behavior, 95–96
   snapping behavior, 92
   thunderphobia, 96–97
proteins in diet, 43
puppies
   activities for, 101
   adopting, 16
   encouraging, 86
   feeding, 43
   grooming, 58
   health care for, 118
   house training, 77–78
   veterinary care, 115

Q
quick-release collars, 30–31

Photo Credits

6493866629 (Shutterstock): 46

Jacqueline Abromeit (Shutterstock): 42

Joan Balzarini: 87

Donna Barr: 60, 115

Mary Burlingame: 18, 23, 95, 119

Dumitrescu Ciprian-Florin (Shutterstock): 121

Norma Cornes (Shutterstock): 4

EcoPrint (Shutterstock): 15

Freddy Eliasson (Shutterstock): 50

George Fairbairn (Shutterstock): 32 (bottom)

Jean M. Fogle@jeanmfogle.com: 9, 12, 17, 26, 40,
   77, 80, 89, 98, 102, 107, 112, 117, 124

Studio Foxy (Shutterstock): 64

HTuller (Shutterstock): 34

Rafa Irusta (Shutterstock): 59

Eric Isselée (Shutterstock): 1, 22, 25, 39
   (bottom), 62,

Laila Kazakevica (Shutterstock): 52

Kinetic Imagery (Shutterstock): 49

Mary Jo Jome: 65

Sandra Kemppainen (Shutterstock): 96

James Klotz (Shutterstock): 38, 44

Neil Kresal: 48

mitzy (Shutterstock): 68

Carole Oinonen: 67

Iurii Osadchi (Shutterstock): 29

Robert Pearcy: 84, 93

Ron Regan: 61, 128

Tina Rencelj (Shutterstock): 72

Shutterstock: 32 (top)

MAGDALENA SZACHOWSKA (Shutterstock): 69

Hedser van Brug (Shutterstock): 36

Cindy Victor: 6

Aleksandar Vozarevic (Shutterstock): 45

Monica Wisniewska (Shutterstock): 131

ene (Shutterstock): 132

All other photos courtesy of TFH archives

Dedication

For my Greyhounds, Minnie and Bruce, and their dad, Gary, whose love makes our world go round.

Acknowledgments

For their generous help with this book, I am grateful to Rodger Barr, DVM (Northern Lights Greyhound Adoption); Kristin Block (Block Sporthounds), licensed inseminator; Laurel Drew (El-Aur Greyhounds), breeder, trainer, Greyhound Club of America archivist; William E. Feeman III, DVM (Greyhound Adoption of Ohio); Michael W. Fox, DVM, syndicated columnist, member of the Royal College of Veterinary Surgeons; Donna Kelley (Cyrano Hounds), breeder; Jo Langer (Nittany Greyhounds); Lee Livingood (Clever Companions), Certified Dog Behavior Consultant, International Association of Animal Behavior Consultants (IAABC); Suzanne Stack, DVM (Arizona Adopt a Greyhound); and Howard Steinberg Ph.D., whose expert advice I have relied on through the years.

About the Author

Cindy Victor is the author of *A Heart for the Hermit Kingdom*, a Korea-based historical romance novel; *Covenant with Death*, a suspense novel; four contemporary romance novels; and the Greyhound novels *Leo: A Greyhound's Tale* and *Leo in China: A Greyhound's 2nd Tale*. Her short stories and articles have appeared in literary reviews, newspapers, and magazines, including *Celebrating Greyhounds* and *The Pet Press*. Cindy lives in Minnesota and volunteers for the Animal Humane Society.